Bitter Grounds:

Roots of Revolt

in El Salvador

by Liisa North

between the lines

©December 1981 Between The Lines

2nd printing June 1982

Published by: Between The Lines
427 Bloor St. W.
Toronto, Ontario, Canada

Typeset by: Dumont Press Graphix
97 Victoria St. N.
Kitchener, Ontario, Canada

Chapter 7 copyright © Tim Draimin

Printed and Bound in Canada by:
The Alger Press Limited

Between The Lines receives financial assistance
from the Ontario Arts Council and the Canada Council.

Canadian Cataloguing in Publication Data

North, Liisa L., 1940-
Bitter grounds

Bibliography: p. i

ISBN 0-919946-24-0 (bound)
ISBN 0-919946-25-9 (pbk)

1. El Salvador — Politics and government.
2. El Salvador — Economic conditions.

I. Title.
FI486.N67   972.84   C82-094021-6

Distributed in the U.S.A. by:
Lawrence Hill and Co.,
Westport, Conn.

Distributed in Britain by:
ZED Press,
57 Caledonia Road,
London

Table of Contents

Appendices

Tables

Illustrations

Preface

Through my work with the Toronto Committee of Solidarity with the People of El Salvador (COSPES), I've often been asked to recommend good general information books and articles on the background to the civil war in that Central American country. Colleagues at York University and the University of Toronto have also enquired about easily accessible and comprehensive readings they might assign in classes.

While trying to answer these requests, I discovered that although a large number of excellent scholarly works on specific aspects of El Salvador's development are available, a synthetic overview remained to be written. With the encouragement of friends, I have attempted to fill this void, and *Bitter Grounds* is the result. It is based almost entirely on secondary sources, on the most authoritative, scholarly works available in English and Spanish. It thus tries to make their findings accessible to a broader audience. Much of chapter 6, which deals with contemporary events, relies primarily on journalistic sources and the reports of organizations concerned with human rights issues.

I want to thank all the authors whose work I have used extensively in writing this synthesis. They are indicated in the Bibliography. Tanya Korovkin conducted an efficient bibliographic search and helped prepare the political chronology included in Appendix I. She also read the first draft of the book, along with Alison Acker, Tim Draimin and Louis Lefeber, all of whom provided valuable criticism and suggestions for revisions. Tim Draimin has also provided a final chapter that briefly examines the history of Canada's relations with El Salvador and explores the restraints that have prevented the federal government from applying a consistent and independent policy. Finally, the editorial work and substantive commentary of Robert Clarke and Heather McArthur have greatly improved the readability of the text. I am, of course, responsible for the final version.

L.N.,
Toronto, December 1981.

8

Introduction 1

El Salvador, one of the smallest and least known countries in the western hemisphere, is also one of the poorest and most densely populated. It has in addition one of the most distorted and inegalitarian systems of social, political and economic organization in Latin America. For over a century, land ownership and power have been vested in a small oligarchy, backed by repressive military forces and vigilante squads. Peasants have been dispossessed of their land — forced to accept seasonal work on large estates for below subsistence wages or to migrate to the country's most isolated areas and to neighbouring Honduras. Unemployment, malnutrition, illiteracy, torture and death are the constant companions of the rural and urban poor who have no chance for economic or cultural improvement under the current Military-Christian Democratic junta. This desperate situation, coupled with escalating repression, has driven four-fifths of El Salvador's population to support guerrilla or popular front organizations fighting against the corrupt and repressive regime that continues to withhold the necessary social and economic transformation. By early 1980, a full-scale civil war was raging in the country.

This, however, is not how either the Reagan administration or the mass media told the story in January 1981 when, following a long tradition of intervention in Latin America, the United States sent military training teams and $25 million in arms to bolster the current junta. Speaking for the new Republican government, U.S. Secretary of State Alexander Haig rationalized rapidly escalating military assistance to El Salvador and other Central American dictatorships by denying the indigenous causes and leadership of the rebellion. In March, Haig branded the revolutionary opposition as part of a Moscow-designed "four-phased operation" for the "ultimate takeover of Central America".[1]*

* Numbered notes appear at the end of each chapter. For more details on sources, see Bibliography.

Even a Salvadorean official was taken aback by these simplistic statements and commented, "The Secretary of State has an incredible imagination."[2] The public outcry provoked inside and outside the United States by the Secretary of State's aggressive and distorted declarations forced the Reagan administration to adopt a more circumspect language. Assistant Secretary of State for Inter-American Affairs, Thomas O. Enders, on July 16, acknowledged the civil war was "Salvadorean in its origins"; however, he simultaneously outlined a U.S. policy that had not changed in substance: continued military and economic assistance to the junta in power, nominally headed by civilian Christian Democrat José Napoleón Duarte.[3]

The U.S. administration and mass communications media have portrayed the Salvadorean regime as centrist and reformist, under fire from extremists on the left and right. In his July declaration, Enders argued that the "great majority" of the Salvadorean population has "welcomed the political and social changes" that supposedly had been put into effect during the previous eighteen months. He pointed to the junta's agrarian reform law and announced constituent assembly and presidential elections in 1982 and 1983 as reflective of a serious and potentially viable effort to establish "a more democratic system". Enders also condemned Cuba and Nicaragua for fuelling an arms traffic that sustains the guerrillas, thus implicitly asking the public to believe that if it were not for outside support, the revolutionary offensive would crumble.

What Enders failed to reveal was that the social and political changes remain promises, not facts: the junta's agrarian reform law has so far profited few but the military officers responsible for its implementation and, unless suicidal, no socially progressive forces would dare participate in the "free" elections of 1982 or 1983. It is precisely the progressive forces that have come face to face with the current regime's policy of "selective extermination." As for the revolutionary offensive, its stability is guaranteed by the breadth of its support base throughout the country.

While the misinformation, half-truths and outrageous distortions of the Reagan administration have appeared on the front pages, the reasoned arguments and evidence of former Duarte government officials and independent observers are buried in congressional subcommittee hearing reports, in low-circulation newsletters published by various church and academic associations or, occasionally, in the back pages of newspapers. For example, the testimony provided by a former Salvadorean land reform official, Leonel Gómez,* to the U.S. House of Representatives Subcommittee on Inter-American Affairs, placed all the arguments concerning the centrist and reformist character of the Salvadorean government into question. Gómez, who is not a supporter of

---

* Mr. Gómez was forced to flee for his life and seek asylum in the United States in early 1981.

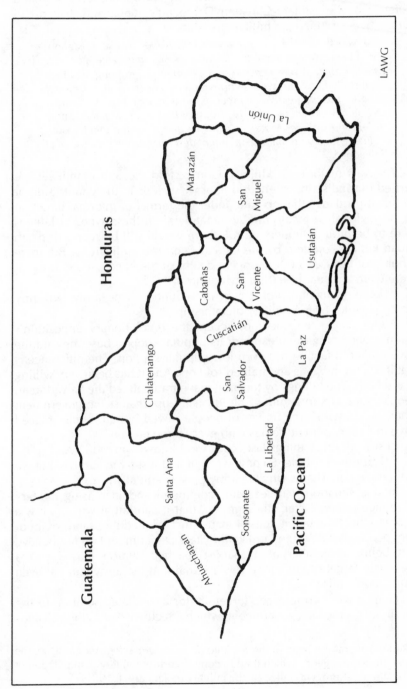

Map 1. Departments of El Salvador.

the revolutionary opposition, described the corruption, repression and violence of the Military-Christian Democratic junta, and the cost in human lives of American military assistance:

> I ask you this, if the government in El Salvador was serious about corruption, would Viera be dead?* . . . And the same goes for whether that government is serious about controlling violence against civilians. If it were, who would be under arrest — Colonel Majano, the progressive member of the [October 15, 1979] junta, or Colonel Moran, head of the Treasury Police? . . . Majano is now in jail and Colonel Moran is still free and directing the Treasury Police, which your State Department describes as the Gestapo of El Salvador.[4]

The vast majority of killings, Gómez told the Subcommittee, are carried out indiscriminately during army sweeps in the countryside or by "death squads" that operate under the formal or informal direction of the regional or local army commanders. "If these types of killings were to be brought under control, there would still be scores of death squad killings, ordered by the radical right in the oligarchy. But there would not be over 5,000 innocent deaths at the hands of the army, as there were last year [1980] in my country."

"The fundamental problem in my country is the army, an army which presides over a military dictatorship."[5]

Although Gómez does not accept the revolutionary opposition's claims concerning the breadth of its popular support base, he said the government in fact enjoys even less popular support. The difference is that it has "more guns and trained soldiers. And it has been very willing to use both. The killings by the army have traumatized the Salvadorean people. One is very cautious about rising up against the government when one has seen the bodies of people sawed in half, bodies placed alive in battery acid or bodies with every bone broken.

"I saw all those things last year. And I know who did it. And so do the Salvadorean people. So now we wait and just try to survive. But we will remember. That is why the army must eventually lose."[6]

In this situation, Gómez said, continued and increasing military assistance in effect "tells the army . . . that it can kill at will. . . . It is a signal to the army that it doesn't matter that it killed thousands of innocent people last year [and unlike the State Department I do not believe that being a member of a Marxist teacher's union makes you a legitimate target of violence]. It is a signal that the army can kill even more people this year."[7]

Gómez went on to argue forcefully for a mediated solution to the conflict. This the U.S. government, which effectively keeps the Salvado-

* Rodolfo Viera, the head of the Instituto de Transformación Agraria (ISTA), the agrarian reform agency which tried to control corrupt military manipulation of agricultural reform, was killed by the military on January 4, 1981.

Source: David Browning, *El Salvador: Landscape and Society.*

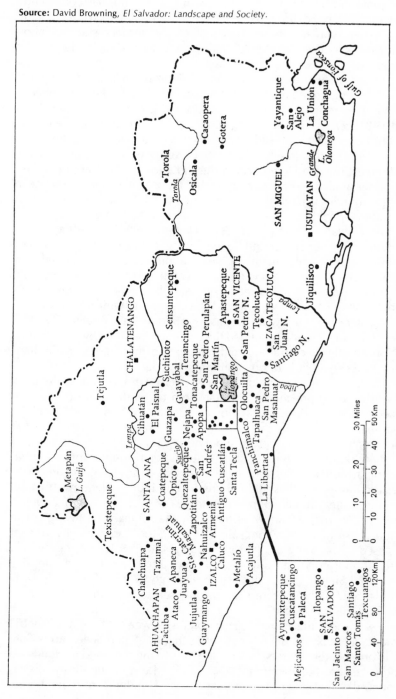

Map 2. Principal place-names.

rean junta in power by providing it with military aid, has consistently rejected. It was Ed Broadbent, leader of Canada's New Democratic Party (NDP), who led the most recent of the unsuccessful mediation efforts on behalf of the international organization of social democratic parties.

The testimony presented by Leonel Gómez is not isolated or unique. Equally strong condemnations have been made by a large number of people who resigned from the Salvadorean government during 1980 and 1981 (see Chapter 6 and Appendix I). In a similar vein, the former Archbishop of San Salvador, Oscar Arnulfo Romero, assassinated in March 1980 by rightist extremists with close connections to the military, asked the Christian Democrats in the junta to "analyze not only their intentions, which no doubt are good, but the real effect their presence in the government is having. Their presence is covering up, especially at the international level, the repressive character of the present regime."[8]

The allegations of the U.S. State Department's "White Paper" on "Communist Interference in El Salvador" were also widely publicized in the American and Canadian periodical press. Reporters and editors, without analyzing the documents, which purported to prove "a textbook case of indirect armed aggression by Communist powers" in Central America, simply presented the Reagan administration's assertions. Later, when a few investigative reporters and, finally, The Wall Street Journal, actually examined the evidence provided by the administration and discovered that it did not support the charges made, their findings received little or no attention in the daily press.[9]

The press and governments of western Europe and some Latin American governments did question both the authenticity of the supposedly captured documents appended to the "White Paper", and the discrepancies between the Reagan administration's charges and the documents presented to prove them during Washington's unsuccessful February diplomatic blitz to obtain international support for its Central American policies. Regrettably, the Canadian government, unlike its western European allies, did not conduct an independent investigation into the matter. Initially opposed to increasing American military intervention, External Affairs Minister Mark MacGuigan, following a late January visit to Washington, said that while the Canadian government opposed the sending of offensive weapons to El Salvador, he "would certainly not condemn any decision the U.S. takes to send offensive arms".[10] Since then, the Canadian government has "quietly acquiesced" to U.S. aggression and refused to support the mediation efforts of the NDP leader.

Meanwhile, the danger of the spread of war to the entire Central American region has increased. For example, United States Army Special Forces (Green Berets) officers are now being stationed in Honduran border regions adjacent to El Salvador. The Reagan administration has proposed a doubling of U.S. military aid to Honduras from the present

$5.4 million to $10.7 million for 1982. And the American ambassador to Honduras accuses the 70,000 Salvadorean refugees and the international relief organizations in that country of providing assistance to Salvadorean revolutionaries. Discussing recent Honduran army incursions into refugee camps, a West Point graduate Special Forces officer said: "They [the refugees] have no human rights", just a "right to food and a roof".[11]

While the ominous escalation of U.S. military intervention and the astoundingly repressive character of the Military-Christian Democratic junta are obscured by most of the media coverage,* the public knows even less about social and economic conditions in El Salvador or about the fundamental indigenous causes of the civil war. The war is rooted in local conflicts and problems which date back more than one hundred years. The revolutionary coalition composed of the Democratic Revolutionary Front (FDR) and the Farabundo Martí National Liberation Front (FMLN) proposes to restructure an inequitable social order that condemns approximately three-quarters of the country's population to permanent material and cultural misery. This revolutionary coalition emerged after a long and fruitless struggle to introduce reforms through peaceful electoral means. It represents the majority of the population and a diversity of political tendencies, ranging from social democrats and radical Christians to Marxists of various currents. In the words of Mexican writer and diplomat, Carlos Fuentes:

> A revolution of complex composition — Catholic, agrarian and nationalist in its roots, but also with strong Marxist, democratic Christian and social-democratic demands, with militant students and accountants, printers and bank clerks — has claimed the right to do for El Salvador what has not been achieved in nearly five centuries: the abolition of colonialism and at the very least the creation of a few conditions that might permit some evolution of the political structure.
>
> They have met the army. . . . For the army is the only obstacle standing between the congealed colonialism that feeds its own vicious circle and any form of evolutionary democracy.[12]

El Salvador suffers from the dubious distinction of having the oldest continuous sequence of military rule in Latin America. The army has governed directly since 1931, enforcing the interests of a narrow economic elite, the coffee export oligarchy which established its dominance in the late nineteenth century.

The history of the country can be summarized as a series of dispossessions by this oligarchy of the great majority of the population from the sources of a livelihood. In the countryside, first the expansion of

* There have been some notable exceptions, especially in the Canadian media. See, for example, *Maclean's* (June 15, 1981) as well as some articles in *The Globe and Mail* and *Toronto Star*.

coffee exports and later the expansion of cotton and sugar production (also for export) drove rural peoples off lands they had cultivated with food crops. Then, following the Second World War, the mechanization of export production reduced the numbers of labourers needed on the estates of the oligarchy. By the 1970s, the majority of the rural population had access to neither land nor regular employment. In the cities, capital-intensive industrialization in the 1950s and 1960s, increasingly under the auspices of U.S.-based multinational corporations, failed to provide gainful employment opportunities. The armies of poor and unemployed thus grew in both the shantytowns of the cities and in the rural hamlets.

The few who controlled the productive process grew immensely rich. Their individualistic pursuit of private gain and resistance to socio-economic reforms has led to the collective social and political catastrophe of civil war. The military, which has enforced the interests of the oligarchy, developed into a repressive caste which closed off the possibilities of a democratic political opening. In this the United States also played a material and ideological role through military aid and counter-insurgency training programmes established in the wake of the Cuban Revolution as a counterpart to the Alliance for Progress.

Notes

[1] *Newsweek* (March 30, 1981).
[2] *Ibid.*
[3] *The New York Times* (July 17, 1981).
[4] Subcommittee on Inter-American Affairs (March 5 and 11, 1981), pp. 196-197.
[5] *Ibid.*
[6] *Ibid.*, p. 198.
[7] *Ibid.*, p. 199.
[8] Inter-Church Committee on Human Rights in Latin America (ICCHRLA) (July-August 1980), p. 29.
[9] See Maslow and Arana (1981); *Latin America Weekly Report* (LAWR) (June 12, 1981); *Central America Update* (March 1981).
[10] *The Globe and Mail* (March 3, 1981).
[11] *The New York Times* (August 9, 1981).
[12] Fuentes (August 1981), p. 33.

"Liberal Revolution": Establishment of a Coffee Republic 2

I n 1881 and 1882 the Salvadorean state issued a series of decree laws
that would have a dramatic effect on the country's social structure.
The new legal order set out by the decrees recognized only private
property and thereby abolished the peasantry's traditional communal
forms of landownership, the *ejidos* and *tierras comunales.**

This abolition of common lands as a legally recognized form of
property eventually meant the dispossession from their homes — and
means of livelihood — of the great majority of the rural population. In
the following decades, more than a quarter of El Salvador's land area
and a much greater proportion of its fertile land were taken from the
peasantry and concentrated in the hands of an aggressive and innova-
tive oligarchy that had gained political power in the 1870s.[1]

In principle, the new legal order was established in the name of
national progress and modernity. In fact, it was designed to advance the
interests of the ruling oligarchy. Members of this oligarchy considered
the ownership of communal land a barrier to economic development,
which they equated with private property and with increasing the cultivation of commercial crops, particularly coffee. The peasantry, on the
other hand, was identified as backward and Indian, incapable of
responding to new market opportunities. Although El Salvador's population was in fact racially mixed or *mestizo*, in the rural areas Indian
cultural organization and languages had survived to the late nineteenth
century. Now, along with the abolition of the traditional economic
organization of the peasant community, the Indian cultural legacy was
derogated.

All these changes formed part of the Liberal Revolution that spread
through the Central American isthmus during the second half of the

---

* *Ejidos* and *tierras comunales* refer to two different forms of communal or
collective forms of landownership dating from Spanish colonial rule.

17

nineteenth century and created the foundations of the contemporary socio-economic and political structures of the region.

The Liberal Land Laws and Dispossession of the Peasantry

In accord with the rising Liberal philosophy, the preamble to the first abolition decrees of February 26, 1881, read:

> The existence of lands under the ownership of Comunidades* impedes agricultural development, obstructs the circulation of wealth, and weakens family bonds and the independence of the individual. Their existence is contrary to the economic and social principles that the republic has adopted.[2]

There is no doubt that during the previous decade El Salvador's peasants had been slower than the country's large landowners in increasing coffee production to take advantage of growing opportunities in international markets. The Salvadorean state had been promoting coffee production for export to substitute for the declining international demand for *indigo,* the country's traditional export earner. But however positively the communal peasantry might have responded to this push — and peasants did respond, although slowly — the possibilities for competing with private estate owners were severely limited. Coffee plants require a five-year period of maturation before the first fruit can be harvested and sold. Peasant farmers, without access to credit and other resources, couldn't wait that long; they couldn't affort to divert the use of their land away from the production of traditional subsistence crops.

By deciding to abolish communal forms of property and to rely on the private estate owners to expand coffee production, the Salvadorean state effectively closed off the possibility of a more egalitarian and democratic path to capitalist development that could have been based, as in Canada or the United States, on widespread access to income-earning property in the rural areas. As David Browning notes, peasant communities *had begun* to produce coffee by 1881,

> and had these local communities been allowed time to complete this conversion on their own land and to sell the first harvest of coffee, the economic and social development of the country might have been very different.[3]

In principle, the new land legislation permitted peasants to acquire private title to plots on former communal lands. Instructions concerning the process for obtaining titles "were published in the national press and one is left to guess how many illiterate villagers realized what actions they should take to safeguard their rights".[4]

In practice, over the course of the following decades, those lands were taken over by the land-hungry large-estate owners and wealthy

---

* *Comunidades* refers to peasant villages with communal lands, either *ejidos* or *tierras comunales* or both.

urban commercial groups anxious to expand production and increase their incomes from sales on booming international markets. Most communal land and the greatest population densities were to be found precisely in the western and central highland areas most suitable for coffee production.[5]

But the actual process of peasant dispossession had begun, in fact, before the 1881/1882 land laws. Legal chicanery, the operations of the market place (for instance, foreclosures on loans for which land had been presented as collateral) and violence all played a role in the take-over of peasant land. The peasantry also resisted its conversion into a landless labouring class. Before the widespread peasant rebellion of 1932, which led to the massacre of 30,000 peasants by the state's security forces and the landlords' "White Guards", a series of popular uprisings had taken place in the coffee producing region in 1872, 1875, 1880, 1885 and 1898.[6]

Some small- and medium-sized properties did emerge in the course of this tranformation to private ownership as the only legally-recognized form of access to land. The changes also triggered migrations of dispossessed peasants to the mountainous and less fertile areas in the forested northern departments, or to the malaria-infested coastal lowlands to the south. A few crossed the frontier to Honduras, starting a population movement that was to become increasingly important as the twentieth century progressed. "The peasant cultivator" became "a dispossessed landless wanderer".[7]

As was to be expected, villages located outside the coffee region were less affected by the new laws. Nevertheless, "Most villages lost, to commercial plantations, all rights of ownership and use of their common lands" and a small number of wealthy landowners consolidated ever larger tracts into their own hands (see Maps 3 and 4).[8] The dominant group of interrelated landowning families that emerged from this process eventually came to be referred to as "los Catorce" or "The Fourteen". Although the wealthiest coffee producers, processors and exporters numbered more than fourteen, the exaggeration is based on a clearly identifiable pattern of extreme inequality in landownership and the concentration of political power in the hands of the few. The continued use of the term up to the present date is also appropriate, although not statistically accurate, in its emphasis on the narrowness of the contemporary elite and the rigidity of the country's class and political power structures.

The Constitution of a Dependent Export Economy

In narrow economic terms, the Liberal Revolution in production could be viewed as a success. It led to "more efficient and intensive use of the land".[9] The wealth of the nation and, most of all, the wealth of coffee producers increased tremendously as the value of coffee exports moved up from $2.9 million in 1881 to $21.9 million in 1916. From constituting approximately 50 per cent of exports in 1882 , coffee dominated the economy by the turn of the century, making up 76 per cent of exports by 1901 and remaining the primary export ever since, reaching a high of 95.5 per cent in 1931.[10] The long-term costs of this economic success, however, were high indeed.

El Salvador became a coffee export economy, a country whose patterns of economic growth and stagnation were to be fundamentally determined by the character and performance of the export sector. Its economic well-being derived directly from how much coffee was produced and sold, and at what prices. In addition to the dangers inherent in dependence on a single export crop, the extreme concentration of land and income within the coffee oligarchy prohibited the development of a strong domestic market. The coffee producers became "luxury importers"[11] while most of the population was denied sufficient income to become consumers of domestically produced agricultural and industrial goods. The wages of agricultural workers in the coffee sector were low even by Third World standards. For example, even in the 1950s, coffee-workers in the Ivory Coast earned 20 per cent more in real terms than workers in El Salvador. Ivory Coast workers received better meals from their employers and each of them was "given a plot of land to cultivate on the side, with a *firm work contract concluded for a whole season*".[12] In El Salvador, while tenancy arrangements for a part of the labour force were also prevalent in the earlier stages of coffee cultivation, landowners always relied on temporary migrant labour during the picking season and eventually eliminated the workers' access to tenant plots where they could cultivate food crops.

As in other export economies, the surplus generated in the export sector, when not spent on luxury consumption, was invested abroad in more profitable opportunities or, eventually, at home in other export industries. This meant that a "thriving export industry could exist for decades alongside a stagnating poverty-stricken domestic sector".[13] In fact, the conversion of land to export production led to periodic declines in domestic food production, accompanied by sharp price increases and eventually substantial food imports.[14] It also led to the widely noted environmental destruction and deforestation of the countryside. As peasants were forced off fertile lands taken over by coffee producers, they had no choice but to cultivate poorer soils and steep inclines in order to meet their basic subsistence needs.

In short, a "vicious cycle" of underdevelopment was set into place in El Salvador, in contrast to the "virtuous cycle" of expanding economic growth based on the widespread ownership of productive property encountered in North America during the same historical period.

Source: David Browning, *El Salvador: Landscape and Society.*

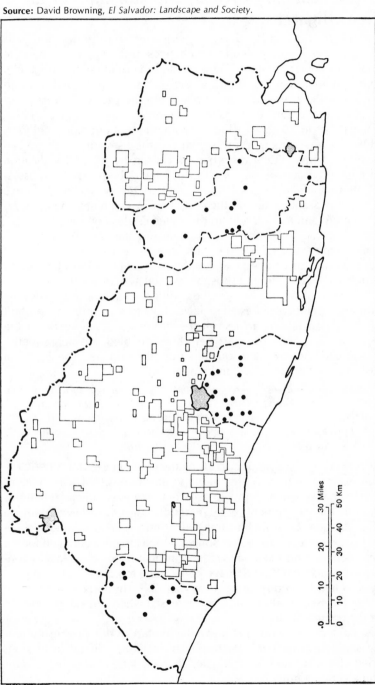

Map 3. Survey of common land. 1879.

The "Exclusionary Civilian Dictatorship" of the Coffee Oligarchy

The transformation in land-tenure structures and production was accompanied by equally significant changes in the nature of the state and political power relations. The state and the ruling coffee oligarchy came to rely more and more on coercion to maintain the stability and expansion of the new economic order. With the peasantry for its part resisting the implementation of Liberal land laws, the period stretching from the 1870s to 1932 was studded with minor and major rebellions. In 1896, the government even recognized the "severity of the social dislocation" and political disturbances caused by its land legislation when it issued a decree intended to slow down the pace of dispossession.[15] But, while it is possible to point to the occasional positive response to peasant protest on the part of the government, the incorporation of more and more land into the coffee estates continued.

Force became necessary to consolidate and maintain the position of the coffee export oligarchy in the rural areas, to guarantee its control of the land as well as of adequate supplies of labour to the plantations, particularly at harvest times. Thus the judicial system was revamped to meet the needs of landlords. After the abolition of *tierras comunales* the government specifically designed legislation to guarantee a constant supply of cheap labour, to recruit the dispossessed for work on the coffee estates. Specifically, the new laws enabled private property-owners to expel tenants and squatters from their estates. The agents of expulsion were the local civil and military authorities.

> *"Agricultural judges"* were appointed in each village and these officials had to keep lists of all day workers, arrange for the capture of those who left an estate before fulfilling their obligations, and to visit private estates regularly to check the need for workers. In this task the local officials were supported by the army.[16]

Accordingly, El Salvador also "took the lead" in Central America in the professionalization of its military institutions.[17] Local officials needed the backing of the army to carry out their new judicial functions. In addition, the government set up rural police forces and eventually, in 1912, a National Guard with rural police functions, to supplement the army. For example, in 1889, a mounted police force was created for the western departments of Ahuachapán, Sonsonate and Santa Ana to control social unrest and "the damage being done to coffee plantations by those who had been dispossessed by them".[18] The force's jurisdiction over dispossessed rural labour later increased when it was expanded to cover the entire country.

The contemporary dominance of the military and police institutions of the state, and the parallel atrophy of civilian political institutions founded on consensus thus originated in the Liberal land policies of the late nineteenth century.

Source: David Browning, *El Salvador: Landscape and Society.*

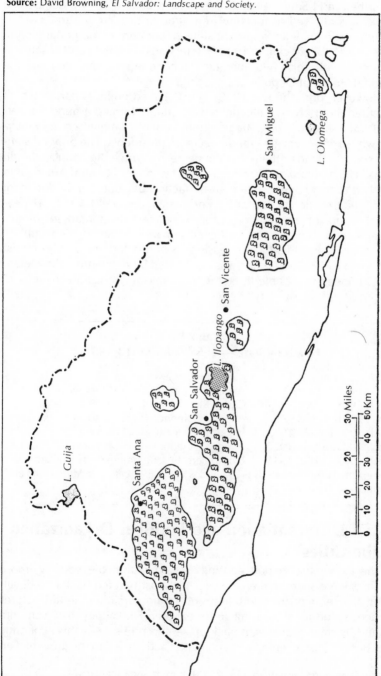

Map 4. Areas of coffee.

While rural union and political organization has been legally proscribed in El Salvador up to the present date, a certain democratic façade was allowed to function from time to time in the urban areas. Urban people made up approximately 20 per cent of the population in 1892 and 21.27 per cent in 1930.[19]* Elections were held and a National Assembly with forty-two members functioned in the form of the National House of Deputies.

However, until the late 1920s, the so-called political parties which presented themselves at elections were simply formed around the personal followings of competing factions of the dominant coffee oligarchy, whose members governed directly as presidents. The only substantial issue that divided them was the degree to which the country should oppose U.S. military and economic penetration into Central America. In response to this issue, a nationalistic faction became briefly dominant during the presidency of Manuel Enrique Araujo (1911-1913). The essential nature of the system, in the words of Salvadorean sociologist Rafael Guidos Véjar, was an "exclusionary civilian dictatorship".[20] One series of presidential successions is particularly revealing of this: from 1913 to 1927 the office was dominated by one family, the Meléndez Quiñónez (see Table I). Not without reason, Salvadoreans refer to the period as "the dynasty".

Table I
Heads of State — El Salvador (1913-1931)

Feb. 1913 to July 1914	Carlos Meléndez
July 1914 to Feb. 1915	Alfonso Quiñónez (Carlos' brother-in-law)
March 1915 to Dec. 1918	Carlos Meléndez
Dec. 1918 to Feb. 1923	Alfonso Quiñónez (same as above)
March 1919 to Feb. 1923	Jorge Meléndez (Carlos' brother)
March 1923 to Feb. 1927	Alfonso Quiñónez (same as above)
March 1927 to Feb. 1931	Pío Romero Bosque (imposed by the family)

Source: cited from Torres-Rivas by Guidos Véjar, *El Ascenso de Militarismo en El Salvador*, p. 76.

Social Differentiation and Political Organization in the Cities

To the extent that export earnings stayed within the country, those earnings were spent in the cities, for the most part fed back into developing the service, transportation and communications infrastructures needed for further expanding coffee exports. The money also went into expanding state activities to back up — and preserve — this economic direction. The quickening pace of market activity led to the growth of an

* The criterion for "urban area" is 2,500 or more inhabitants.

urban middle class of public employees, commercial middlemen and owners of small enterprises. An urban working class also emerged, made up of people employed in small- and medium-sized manufacturing and food-processing establishments, in construction, commerce and transport.

Within the limits of the "exclusionary civilian dictatorship", mutual aid organizations and associations were also able to develop in the cities, particularly in the capital, San Salvador. These bodies included cooperatives, savings associations, charities and clubs. In short, groups of workers, artisans and students organized to represent their interests before the government. In 1917 there were at least forty-five such associations. In 1918 a Workers' Congress, with 200 delegates, was held in the town of Armenia. And in 1920 the first strikes in the country's history took place.

Not the least of the opportunities available for upward mobility were the military and police forces which, with their professionalization, were becoming respected institutions. Spanish and Chilean missions were contracted for organizing a professional structure and system of education for the army.[21] The National Guard was organized in 1912 under the direction of Spanish officers, "with detachments in most rural towns and villages" and a primary task of "maintaining political control in rural areas".[22] These professionalized military institutions "became an important avenue to prestige and power" for the emerging middle class.[23] And, in addition to their obvious repressive functions, the institutions played an important function of political socialization. With the establishment of compulsory military service for all sectors of the population, "the army [became] a means of providing some education to the masses, especially along lines which would promote support for the modernization policies [of the export oligarchy] and nationalize *esprit* and support behind the government".[24]

In summary, while coffee export earnings continued to grow, the urban economy could also expand, thereby creating the social conditions that permitted a circumscribed political democratization in the cities and towns of El Salvador. Under boom conditions, the export oligarchy could afford to expand white-collar employment in the civilian and military bureaucracies of the state, to promote infrastructural development and work opportunities in related sectors of the economy, to co-opt opponents and even respond to some of the demands expressed by the associations and organizations of the urban middle and working classes. This was the character of the democratic façade that developed during the "Meléndez Quiñónez dynasty". But none of this applied to the rural areas, where force was employed openly and liberally to dispossess peasants and control the now increasingly landless and miserable labour force.

The Social and Political Philosophy of the Export Oligarchy

Even a brief overview of the establishment of the "coffee republic" of El Salvador would be incomplete without considering the variants of Liberal philosophy and political thought to which the coffee export oligarchy and its supporters in the cities subscribed. In effect, they adopted the politically and socially most regressive and anti-democratic aspects of nineteenth century Liberalism, deriving from the positivism of French sociologist August Comte and the social Darwinism of English sociologist Herbert Spencer.[25]

From Comte, they took over the idea of "republican dictatorship" as a necessity for establishing "order and progress". In the Salvadorean context, this meant, of course, the philosophical rationalization of the undemocratic rule of the coffee export oligarchy as the promoters of economic growth and "positive" material prosperity, and of "scientific" thought applied to increasing production. From the social Darwinists, who applied Darwin's evolutionary theories concerning natural selection to society, they adopted the idea of "natural" inequalities. Specifically, the poor were considered "unfit" and social reform in the form of labour or welfare legislation was opposed since it was thought to interfere with natural selection — the competitive struggle that would elevate the most able or superior members of the species to positions of power and wealth. The fact that the Salvadorean coffee export oligarchy did not operate in an untrammelled competitive struggle but constructed its power with the backing of the state military and police forces did not bother the advocates of these ideas.*

Since the great majority of the Salvadorean population was not only poor but also of Indian or racially-mixed origin, social Darwinism there as well as elsewhere in Latin America during the same historical period took on overtly racist overtones. Native culture was disparaged and rejected. Ironically, but in this context understandably, it was foreigners rather than nationals who began to study the numerous archeological sites of Central America. Turning its back to the indigenous and authentic national culture of the country, the coffee export oligarchy created in the major cities a supposedly cosmopolitan culture, which was "a shallow imitation of more developed areas" of Europe and North America; it was an imitation "notably lacking in indigenous creativity or imagination".[27] This penchant for ostentatious consumption has not lessened

---

* Woodward summarizes: "Clear patterns emerged which reflected [the Liberal oligarchy's] obsession with material development; their anticlericalism; their faith in scientific and technical education; their rejection of the metaphysical; their willingness to postpone political democracy through what Comte called 'republican dictatorships'; their emulation and imitation of northern European and North American values, capital and leadership; and their insensitivity to the desires and needs of the working class."[26]

with the passing of time. As a Salvadorean sociologist puts it, even now members of the ruling oligarchy, with their second homes in Miami, "are provincial, inbred, uncultured, and avaricious, with a taste for the deepest sofas, hi-fi sets with the most knobs, the shiniest cars, and the blondest blondes".[28]

As the European and then the North American became identified with modernity, technology, progress, industry and urbanity — in short, with civilization — the native rural world was regarded and condemned as backward and barbaric. The response of a fictional character in the Salvadorean novel *Ola Roja* to the growing poverty of the rural population in the midst of the Great Depression reflected widely shared views:

> These... are miserable Indians who content themselves with a salary of four reales a day, which is what their indolence is worth, and their ignorance and laziness.... I did all that was possible to better the conditions of the Indians, but didn't accomplish much because of their lack of cooperation.... They speak our language in school, but on leaving revert to Nahuatl.[29]

The rural masses mattered only in terms of the labour they could provide; in other respects, they were considered irrelevant or extraneous to the process of transformation and modernization propelled by the oligarchy's drive to expand exports and foreign trade. The rural population was effectively denied citizenship. This also is a state of affairs that has lasted to the present date. The peasant continues to be an object of derision, despised and regarded as a backward obstacle to development. Attitudes of urban Salvadoreans are reflected in such popular stereotypes as: "Once a *campesino,* always a *campesino....* Give a *campesino* three *colones* a day and he'll spend two and a half on *aguardiente....* Give him five *colones* a day and he'll spend four and a half."[30]*

In summary, the basic contours of El Salvador's contemporary socio-economic and political power structure, and its cultural organization, were set into place during the period extending from the 1880s to the Great Depression. These consisted of: a single-crop primary export economy, with all its implications for maintaining the "vicious cycle" of underdevelopment; a narrow ruling class which concentrated land and export earnings into its own hands, and as a consequence blocked the development of a strong national economy, which could have emerged only if the mass of the population had sufficient incomes to purchase goods in the marketplace; a political system that relied on coercion for maintaining the dominant position of export interests and therefore encouraged the exaggerated development of the military and

---

* *Campesino* means peasant. *Aguardiente* is the local moonshine, distilled from corn.

police institutions of the state and the parallel weak development of political institutions to generate consensus, particularly in the rural areas; and finally, a socio-political philosophy among the dominant export oligarchy (shared by allied sectors of the urban middle class) that was profoundly anti-democratic, racist and oriented to the imitation of the values and socio-economic organization of the advanced capitalist societies.

Notes

[1] Browning (1971), p. 190; Menjívar (1980), p. 23, estimates the area affected as "no less than 40 per cent of the national territory".

[2] Quoted in Browning (1971), p. 205. The following discussion of the transformation of the land tenure structure relies heavily on Browning's authoritative work, pp. 174-221.

[3] *Ibid.*, p. 189.

[4] *Ibid.*, p. 209.

[5] Durham (1979), p. 34.

[6] Menjívar (1980), p. 69; and Durham (1979), p. 43.

[7] Browning (1971), p. 219.

[8] *Ibid.*, p. 214.

[9] *Ibid.*, p. 216.

[10] In 1911, coffee exports made up 73 per cent of total exports; in 1921, 80 per cent; in 1931, 95.5 per cent; in 1941, 79 per cent. See Guidos Véjar (1980), p. 49; and Browning (1971), p. 222.

[11] Levin (1960), p. 10.

[12] White (1973), p. 123, emphasis added.

[13] Levin (1960), p. 10.

[14] Durham (1979), p. 36.

[15] *Ibid.*, p. 43.

[16] Browning (1971), p. 217.

[17] Woodward (1976), p. 169.

[18] Browning (1971), p. 218.

[19] Durham (1979), p. 28.

[20] Guidos Véjar (1980), p. 111.

[21] *Ibid.*, p. 125.

[22] Arnson (March 1980), p. 5.

[23] Woodward (1976), p. 170.

[24] *Ibid.*

[25] *Ibid.*, pp. 155-156.

[26] *Ibid.*, p. 56.

[27] *Ibid.*, p. 173.

[28] Quoted in Buckley (June 22, 1981), p. 56.

[29] Cited by Anderson (1971), p. 17.

[30] Buckley (June 22, 1981), p. 68.

Peasant Rebellion of 1932

3

W ith the onset of the Great Depression, all the most brutal characteristics of the system of oligarchic domination came to the forefront. The demand for coffee on the international markets collapsed and prices fell dramatically. With coffee no longer in demand, the limited possibilities of the peasantry to obtain even temporary work faded away. Having already lost their land, peasants now also lost the opportunity to work — even if it had been for low wages and under poor conditions.

The peasant response to this increased misery was an extensive revolt, which broke out in the coffee-producing areas of the western and central highlands in January 1932. The state and landlords responded to this with extreme measures: 30,000 peasants, as well as some urban workers and students, were massacred by military and police forces and landowners' "White Guards". The subsequent political development of the country was profoundly affected by these events; they effectively terminated rule by "exclusionary civilian dictatorship" and established the dictatorial rule of the military, which has held sway ever since.

The Rebellion of 1932, however, didn't just happen as an isolated event. As we've seen, it followed a long history of peasant resistance. In fact, it derived from the entire history of peasant dispossession since the 1870s and 1880s, as well as from specific developments of the 1920s. During the latter decade two contrasting processes, both related to a new expansion of coffee production (See Tables II and III) were taking place. On the one hand, the tremendous profits derived from exports activated the urban economy; in this prosperous situation, a noticeable democratization took place in the cities. It eventually led to the only free presidential election held in El Salvador's history. On the other hand, the same process of export expansion led to a second wave of peasant dispossession and increasing political repression in the rural areas.[1]

29

Table II
Coffee Exports — El Salvador (1922-1935)

Year	Kilograms	Value in Colones	Average Price Per Quintal	% of Total Exports Quantity	Value
1922	43,078,801	28,574,169	30.51	78.31	87.68
1923	41,994,124	29,836,825	32.68	79.89	86.16
1924	48,808,831	45,438,045	42.82	87.40	93.23
1925	32,064,286	30,364,765	43.56	76.46	89.91
1926	50,626,338	46,720,335	42.45	84.67	94.82
1927	36,202,789	25,237,402	32.07	78.45	89.16
1928	53,108,628	45,482,131	39.39	82.73	92.76
1929	46,782,617	48,090,450	33.52	85.15	92.56
1930	58,621,408	23,914,481	18.75	88.11	87.55
1931	54,630,848	21,695,441	18.27	94.10	95.46
1932	39,654,894	12,867,077	14.92	94.78	92.16
1933	56,189,269	19,512,556	15.97	90.55	96.14
1934	49,866,286	22,824,125	21.05	95.54	94.91
1935	50,067,209	24,228,376	22.26	94.14	89.43

Source: Guidos Véjar, *El Ascenso de Militarismo en El Salvador*, p. 102. Cited from Ernesto Richter, *Proceso de Acumulación en La Formación Socio-Política Salvadoreña* (San José: CSUCA, Mimeo, 1976).

Table III
Area Cultivated in Coffee — El Salvador (1921-1933)
(Hectares)

Year	Area Cultivated in Coffee
1921	57,000
1924	81,000
1931	93,000
1933	95,000

Source: Guidos Véjar, *El Ascenso de Militarismo en El Salvador*, p. 102. Cited from León Zamose, *The Definition of a Socio-Economic Formation: El Salvador on the Eve of the Great World Economic Depression* (Manchester: University of Manchester, Mimeo, 1977).

Socio-Economic Diversification and a Limited Urban "Democratization"

During the 1920s, coffee prices remained high, and total production grew as more and more land was devoted to cultivation of the one crop. By then, processors and exporters had begun to obtain a greater proportion of the surplus generated by coffee exports, improving their positions vis-à-vis the producers. From this new position of strength, these groups — along with immigrant capital* and wealthy members of the urban elite, especially those engaged in banking, insurance and commerce — began to promote a more diversified economy. Accordingly, they encouraged the production of cotton and henequen and backed the beginnings of industrial development, particularly in textile manufacturing.

The financial needs of these new activities — and the infrastructure to support them — were more than local money could handle, with the result that U.S. investment became important in the Salvadorean economy for the first time. U.S. investment had added up to only $1.8 million in 1908, steadily increasing to $6.6 million in 1914 and $12.8 million in 1919. But in the 1920s investment from the United States almost doubled, reaching $24.8 million by 1929.[3]†

This investment was concentrated in mining and railways (sectors in which the United States displaced British capital) as well as in banking, public utilities and construction. Canadians also invested in the Salvadorean economy at the time: the San Salvador Electric Light Co., controlled by International Power Ltd., was established in 1924 and continued to operate until 1977 when it was purchased by the government.

All this activity brought unprecedented prosperity to the urban areas, particularly San Salvador, since, as before, that portion of export earnings not invested abroad was, on the whole, invested or spent in the urban economy: in the diversification of commerce, finance and manufacturing, in the salaries of state employees and the provision of some public services by a state that was coming to play a larger and larger role in the economy. It was in this context that a "democratization" began to take place in the cities, a process that eventually had its most profound repercussions in the rural areas — where, ironically, its reverse was being experienced. There, a second and brutal wave of peasant dispossession was occurring as coffee cultivation expanded to new lands and smaller properties were absorbed by the larger estates.[5] At the same time, cotton and henequen production was also displacing subsistence crops, so it became necessary for the country to import sizable quantities of food.[6]

* European immigrants arrived in El Salvador, as they did to other parts of Latin America, in the late nineteenth and early twentieth centuries. Although few in numbers, they played an important role in the economy, initially in commerce, finance and importing and exporting (they possessed a knowledge of foreign markets that gave them a competitive advantage). Later, they also became active in the processing of coffee.[2] Over the following decades they married into and became integrated with the national elites.

† These amounts were, of course, small in comparison to U.S. investment elsewhere in Latin America. In 1929, American investment in Central America as a whole represented 6.9 per cent of its total Latin American investments.[4] Given the small size of the Salvadorean economy, however, even this relatively small investment was important.

By the 1920s, the oligarchy, now more secure and interested in governing with at least a measure of popular support, showed signs of allowing a political opening. To obtain popular support, the government put a certain amount of social legislation on the books in the last part of the decade. But such legislation was implemented only sporadically. More importantly, in 1918, Alfonso Quiñónez, "the veritable organizer of the economic-political system and of the domination of the dynasty", founded what could be considered the country's first political party.[7] Called the *Liga Roja* (or "Red League"), it brought together workers, intellectuals and even a few peasants, offering them "plots of land and wage increases". More ominously, the party also had paramilitary functions: it was utilized to intimidate and to break up the meetings of opposition groups organized by sectors of the oligarchy dissatisfied with the narrow family rule of the Meléndez-Quiñónez dynasty.

The *Liga Roja* was short-lived; autonomous labour and political associations began to appear in the twenties, variously inspired by anarcho-syndicalist thought and the Mexican and Russian Revolutions. This coincided with increased labour militancy: railway workers, shoemakers, tailors, teachers and other groups of workers staged strikes for higher wages and better working conditions between 1919 and 1922. All this activity led to the organization in 1924 of the *Regional de Trabajadores de El Salvador*.* By 1929 the *Regional* had forty-one member unions and small local associations of unions. It eventually brought together approximately 10.6 per cent of the economically active population (artisans, workers and employees), with perhaps as many as 75,000 members, most of them younger workers.[8] As it grew, its leadership changed, from being under the direction of anarcho-syndicalists in its early years, to Marxist control by the late 1920s. Already, in 1925, the *Regional* had affiliated itself to the radically anti-imperialist *Confederación Obrera Centroamericana* (COCA) and the *Confederación Sindical Latinoamericana*. Increasing radical criticism of the way the state operated thus accompanied increasing working class organization, culminating finally in the founding of the Communist Party of El Salvador during the crisis of the Great Depression in 1930.†

Rural Activism and Popular Ideologies

If union organization could take place in the cities, in the rural areas it was still expressly prohibited by law, and even the relatively democratic government of Romero Bosque (1927-1931) specifically "ordered the

* The Regional (Organization) of the Workers of El Salvador.

† It must be emphasized that El Salvador in the 1920s did not have a modern industrial structure. The "workers" organized included artisans and even public employees in addition to labourers in small- and medium-size manufacturing enterprises, in transport and communications, in services and commerce.

persecution and repression of union organizations and of leftist activities in the rural zones".[9] Nevertheless, the political and union activism of urban areas began to spill over into the peasant villages of the western and central highlands, those areas which had borne the brunt of both the first and the second phases of dispossession. Organizers with knowledge or experience of the Mexican Revolution of 1910-1917 and members of the newly-founded Communist Party were particularly active in building up political opposition in the highlands. They had help from landless migrant peasants, who had crowded into the cities in search of employment and carried the new ideas they found there back to the countryside.

Although a Marxist critique of the state was prominent in the political and union activism of the 1920s, Marxism was only one of many heterogeneous ideological currents agitating Salvadorean society, and that heterogeneity continued to be reflected even within the *Regional de Trabajadores*. The most widespread body of critical thought in El Salvador at the time was *vitalismo mínimo* (literally, "minimum vitalism"), expounded by one of the country's foremost intellectuals, Alberto Masferrer, through the journal *Patria*. Masferrer, the founder of the concept, argued that everyone in the society had a right to receive the "vital minimum" of goods and services necessary to live a materially and culturally decent life.

Patria was the most important of the many popular journals published in the 1920s. Breaking away at least partially from the Comtean and social Darwinist positions which had provided the political ideology for the ruling oligarchy and its supporters, Masferrer's journal advocated reform and became "a veritable [political] party, even though it did not have an organizational expression. *Patria* converted itself into a kind of 'national conscience' which advocated progress and social justice in an environment of 'order and peace'."[10]

Salvadorean sociologist Rafael Guidos Véjar, summarizing the content and impact of Masferrer's thought and public advocacy, notes that the man struggled for many long years to change public thinking and open the way for a restructuring of the country's economy. Masferrer became the intellectual most capable of orienting those groups committed to a "silent transformation" of El Salvador. Along with other intellectuals who were also writing in journals and newspapers at the time, Masferrer constructed a political philosophy that differed with the one developed in the "oligarchic society". Véjar states:

> Masferrer created the cultural-ideological conditions for rooting the basic changes which were taking place in Salvadorean social life. In Patria, he succeeded in forging together the thought of the various urban groups which promoted the new industrial, commercial and financial activities which rejuvenated the national structures.

He identifies Masferrer as "neither a revolutionary Marxist nor a utopian socialist", but rather as "an organic intellectual of a bourgeois project / of a progressive form of capitalism / which tried to impose itself on Salvadorean society as a whole". The man was able to unify the chaotic ideologies of urban reform groups under his own eclectic thought, which embraced mysticism, nationalism, and anti-imperialism directed against the United States. He drew these together with his "minimum vitalism", which synthesized "statism", the idea of collaboration among classes, and reformism.[11]

1931: A Presidential Election and a Coup d'État

In this context of energetic political discussion, social ferment and organizational activity, Pío Romero Bosque, the last of the presidents selected by the Meléndez-Quiñónez, decided to hold free elections for the presidency in January 1931. By the time the elections were held, however, the shock waves of the Great Depression were breaking down the fragile structure of El Salvador's export-dependent economy. Understandably, there were those among the oligarchy who doubted the wisdom of Romero Bosque's decision; but the elections went ahead.

Six presidential candidates, backed by political parties organized for the occasion, contested the election. Of these candidates, Arturo Araujo and his *Partido Laborista,* or Labour Party, were by far the most popular. Araujo, a maverick from the ruling oligarchy, had a reputation for treating the workers of his enterprises well. At the first Workers' Congress in 1918, he had been presented with the title "Benefactor of the Working Class in General". In England, where he had studied new agricultural technologies, Araujo had become convinced of the need for industrialization. Not surprisingly, then, his *Partido Laborista* was inspired by its British namesake and Malferrer's socio-political philosophy.

Araujo's popularity ascended with the velocity of the deepening social crisis. Supported by the majority of the urban middle and working classes, the recently organized Communist Party and peasants who were promised an agrarian reform by Labour Party activists, he was elected President, taking office on March 1, 1931. Nine months later, in the midst of popular jubilation, he was deposed by a group of young officers who quickly turned power over to Araujo's appointed Vice-President, General Maximiliano Hernández Martínez.[12]

Araujo and his Labour Party were simply incapable of formulating and implementing policies to deal with the basic problems created by the Depression. The oligarchy, as could be expected, boycotted the new government, withdrawing its experienced administrative personnel from the state bureaucracy. The young Labour Party could not provide knowledgeable, alternative talent. The programme announced on Araujo's inauguration — control over sale of alcoholic beverages, improvements in tax collections, use of the army for carrying out a literacy programme — was in essence a bandaid for controlling a hemorrhage. In the midst of strikes and demonstrations, the demands for drastic and fundamental reforms escalated as hundreds of thousands of workers were left without jobs following a decision by coffee producers not to harvest their crops.Those who still had some form of employment found their wages cut.[13] Salvadorean sociologist Alejandro D. Marroquin "calculated, as a conservative estimate, that unemployment reached 40 per cent for the adult male population of the countryside alone and 15 per cent in the urban areas in 1929, and it later grew, especially in 1930 with the coffee producers' decision not to harvest coffee".[14]

Meanwhile the large coffee processors, producers and exporters had decided to cut their losses by "transferring the weight [of the crisis] to medium and small coffee producers who had to sell their harvest at seventy to eighty per cent below the international price".[15] In short, Araujo's popular base disintegrated — the reforms he was offering were totally inadequate — while neither the *Partido Laborista* nor any other popularly-based group had sufficient organizational capacity or programmatic coherence to hold onto power and formulate a viable alternative to confront the socio-economic crisis.

As a consequence, the popular reaction to the coup carried out by a group of young officers on December 2, 1931, was relief. Even the Communist Party joined in congratulating the officers for carrying out their civic duty and deposing the President who had defrauded his supporters. That there was a certain amount of confusion about the nature and implications of the coup is understandable: the agitation for reform and democratization of the 1920s had elicited positive reactions from the army officer corps, which was recruited from the middle and lower-middle classes. However, the younger "progressive" officers had no more of a programme than the *Partido Laborista* or Masferrer — who had already retired in dismay to self-imposed exile in Guatemala. Effective power devolved rapidly to Hernández Martínez and the top level of the military hierarchy. Those people did have a programme: the imposition of political order to permit the recuperation of the country's economy. That meant coffee production and the defence of the export oligarchy or the coffee producers.

The Peasant Rebellion and the Matanza

While political agitation continued in both the cities and the countryside, Hernández Martínez permitted the holding of already scheduled municipal elections for January 5-10. The Communist Party, as well as other radical groups, presented candidates. Simultaneously, however, the Party, under the influence of the Third International which was then in its "extremist" or "insurrectionist" phase, prepared for a mass uprising. The revolt, which was to achieve the immediate seizure of power, was planned for January 22, 1932.[16] Unfortunately for the Communist Party, the plot was discovered and Party leaders arrested following the municipal elections. As a result, the Party did not play the major role in the peasant uprising that did break out, on January 20. However, because the Communist Party did not effectively control the rural masses — even in the best of circumstances, with its leaders available — it is doubtful that its members would have been able to control and provide direction to the uprising in any case.

The 1932 rebellion was centred in the western-highland, coffee-growing areas and its effective leaders were the Indian *caciques* — or "headmen" — of the villages. Its organizational units were the *cofradías* — the exclusively Indian religious associations. The peasantry in fact had never accepted any organization distinct from the *cofradías*, in spite of the influence of various secular political groups active in the rural areas at the time. The difference, as Guidos Véjar points out, is that the *cofradías* were rooted in indigenous history and social organization:

> The peasants and salaried workers of the western zone, in their majority were of Indian origin and, even when they accepted municipal organization as a local power, they persisted in obeying the caciques of the indigenous communities and the directors of the "cofradías".[17]

The *cofradías* were Catholic associations whose membership was strictly limited to Indians. They were "dedicated to the religious adoration of a single saint or a person of the Trinity", but at the same time mixed pagan and Catholic customs in their adopted rites. They drew the Indian population together in cohesive groups, which thus became the centre of attention for various political bodies seeking to build up support in the rural areas. According to Guidos Véjar:

> The "Liga Roja" had brought them into its activities; priests used them to preach an ideology of resignation and conformity. All the aspirants to the presidency had gone during the 1931 campaign to the jefes or caciques to solicit their support; the Communists had succeeded in influencing them, etc., but none of the politicians who approached them could change the type of organization.[18]

It was, then, the traditional leaders and organizations of the peasantry that provided actual direction to the rebellion in the rural areas.*

The rebellion was specifically located around the former Indian communities of Santa Ana, Ahuachapán and Sonsonate in the departments of the same name.[19] Its headquarters were located in the village of Juayua, whose communal lands had been mostly taken over by large estates even before the 1881 and 1882 land decrees.[20] (See Map 5.)

* Thomas P. Anderson does not fully explain the significance of the *caciques* and *cofradías* in his *Matanza: El Salvador's Communist Revolt of 1932*, though much of his work points in that direction. Anderson focuses on the urban and party influences rather than analyzing the structure of the peasant community. Consequently, his work, while most informative, is also somewhat misleading. Certainly the subtitle is questionable, although the influence of Communist Party organizers, and particularly the dedicated activities of Augustín Farabundo Martí, were important.

Source: Thomas P. Anderson, *Matanza: El Salvador's Communist Revolt of 1932*.

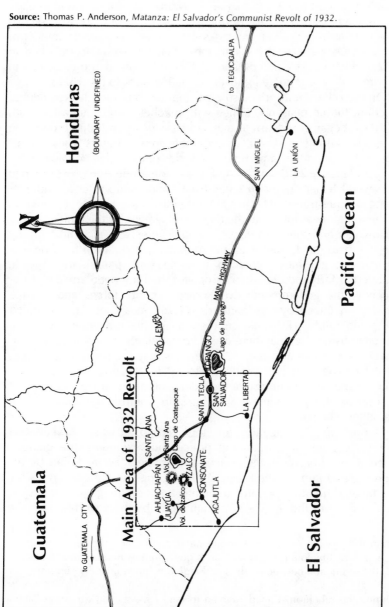

Map 5. Main area of 1932 Peasant Revolt.

These were precisely the areas that had been most severely affected by the dispossessions of the nineteenth century, as well as of the 1920s when coffee cultivators expanded their area of production in response to high prices on the world markets.[21] Moreover, the area had already experienced political unrest during the first wave of dispossession. To these long-term historical processes was added the specific impact of the Great Depression. It is clear, then, that the peasantry rebelled in 1932 to regain possession of lands it rightfully considered its own, and to redress the accumulated grievances dating back to the 1870s.

On the other hand, it is also clear that the rebellion lacked central direction. Indian peasants, armed with machetes and only a few with old rifles, began to occupy estates and *ladino* (non-Indian) towns, in some cases killing local officials and estate administrators. These events happened around the same time as a series of extensive volcanic eruptions, on January 22 ("Volcán de Fuego, Volcán de Agua, Acatonango and several lesser craters in Guatemala" and Izalco in El Salvador),[22] raising the question of whether the eruptions played a role in convincing the Indian peasantry that the day of judgement for the coffee plantation owners and their *ladino* or "white" allies was at hand.* In any case, the peasants lacked even the minimal coordination the Communist Party might have provided if its leaders, particularly Agustín Farabundo Martí and his urban associates, had not been arrested. Consequently, the government's well-armed security forces and "White Guards" organized by the landlords quickly recaptured the occupied towns and lands. The rapid suppression of the movement was also facilitated by the fact that there was no parallel uprising in San Salvador. However extensive and prepared the conspiracy network in the cities might have been, it had been penetrated by the government, as the earlier arrests of Communist Party leaders and other radicals indicates.† As soon as the government was back in control, the *matanza* (or "slaughter") began.

During the occupation of the *ladino* towns, "twenty-one [identifiable] persons, including police, but excluding the guardia, police of the line, customs police, and soldiers" were killed by the machetes and guns of the rebels.[24] During the subsequent repression, an estimated hundred people, at the most, fell on the government side. The estimates of the numbers "slaughtered" by the government range

---

* From the peasant perspective, the hispanicized urban dwellers were white; since, in fact, the country's population is quite homogeneously mixed or *mestizo*, the distinction between Indian and *ladino* is fundamentally cultural.

† During the rebellion, Canada agreed to land a vessel (on a routine Pacific cruise) in El Salvador at the request of the British Foreign Office, which was concerned about possible threats to British lives and property. The Salvadorean government declined the proffered aid.[23]

from 10,000 to 50,000, with 30,000 the most commonly-cited figure. Thomas Anderson has reconstructed the terror in the town of Izalco:

> As most of the rebels, except the leaders, were difficult to identify, arbitrary classifications were set up. All those who were carrying machetes were guilty. All those of a strongly Indian cast of features, or who dressed in a scruffy, campesino costume were considered guilty. To facilitate the roundup, all those who had not taken part in the uprising were invited to present themselves at the comandancía* to receive clearance papers. When they arrived they were examined and those with the above mentioned attributes seized. Tied by the thumbs to those before and behind them, in the customary Salvadorean manner, groups of fifty were led to the back wall of the church of Asunción in Izalco and against that massive wall were cut down by firing squads. In the plaza in front of the comandancía, other selected victims were made to dig a mass grave and then shot, according to one account, from machine guns mounted on trucks. In some cases, women and children refused to leave their menfolk and shared their fate. An old Izalco resident, who was then a soldier in the army, says there is no doubt that the guardia behaved much worse than the rebels, "shooting anyone they came across".[25]

The repression also took on strongly racist characteristics. A *ladino* survivor from the village of Juayua is reported to have said, a few days after the revolt, that "We'd like this race of the plague to be exterminated. . . . It is necessary for the government to use a strong hand. They did it right in North America, having done with them by shooting them in the first place before they could impede the progress of the nation." A February 4, 1932 story in the Salvadorean newspaper, *La Prensa*, was headlined: "The Indian has been, is and will be the enemy of the *Ladino*." The author, a landholder, wrote: "There was not an Indian who was not afflicted with devastating communism. . . . We committed a grave error in making them citizens."[26]

The repression in San Salvador was moderate only in comparison to the terrible excesses in the rural areas. Communist Party leader Augustín Farabundo Martí was executed on February 1, 1932, together with two young associates, Mario Zapata and Alfonso Luna who had been in prison with him when the rebellion took place.

The Aftermath of the Matanza

The democratic opening of the 1920s thus ended in a veritable blood bath in, 1932. All union and political activity was subsequently prohibited by the government; the lively periodical press was closed down. El Salvador entered a political dark age that lasted into the 1940s. As elsewhere in Central America, the Salvadorean government "took on in an organized and official form an entire ideological program which sought to liquidate any manifestation of social protest".[27] This meant

* The military command post.

that any movements that questioned the oligarchic domination of the country were labelled communist and subversive. In both this perception and the attendant policies of repression, El Salvador's rulers received the support of the United States.

In the following years, the events associated with the peasant rebellion and the *matanza* were systematically falsified in the national press. A "history" of peasant barbarism and murderous Communist hordes was manufactured while the officially-sponsored "slaughter" was conveniently forgotten. Year after year, the falsified history was dusted off to provide fresh editorial and newspaper accounts, particularly for those rare occasions when the question of agrarian reform was raised. Salvadorean poet Roque Dalton satirized the consequences of this big lie in an imaginary 1972 opinion survey with typical citizens:

> — Tell me, compañero, what is your opinion about the events of the year 32?
> — What events of the year 32?
> — The year 32 when the Government of General Martínez carried out a violent repression against Salvadorean workers, especially against the peasants, and the dead numbered. . . .
> — Aren't you talking about the slaughter perpetrated by the Communists?
> — Well, what is your opinion?
> — They say that it was terrible. The Indians took up their machetes against the rich and wound up cutting off everybody's head. They say that they were just about to enter San Salvador and that they were going to kill off everyone who wore shoes, not to mention a tie, and that they were going to rape all the women. The slaughter they perpetrated was tremendous. Afterwards, it seems that the communist leaders were shot and everything calmed down. . . .
> — The real events were a bit different, compañero. There really was a massacre. More than thirty thousand dead. But our fellow countrymen and brothers were assassinated by the Army, not the communists. The rebel peasants. . . .
> — Well, look. Are you communists, saying such things?[28]

With the Great Depression, the move towards greater economic diversification that had begun in the 1920s in urban areas was halted. For one thing, the government took measures to protect the incomes of coffee plantation owners, who had been losing ground to the processors and urban commercial and financial groups — the people who had given impetus and provided the investment funds for diversification. The government policies, along with the effects of the depression, brought the closing down of existing enterprises, with a subsequent increase in urban unemployment. In addition, the country was confronted with a 100 per cent reduction in coffee prices in 1932, which meant that the fiscal revenues of the state melted away. As a result, public employees were persuaded to accept a 30 per cent reduction in salaries.[29] Peasants, for their part, fled the political terror and social misery of the coffee zone, migrating to El Salvador's sparsely populated northern departments, to the cities and to Honduras.

Mario Zapata, in an interview a few days before his execution, argued that coffee was responsible for the destruction of the country. Before the age of coffee, Zapata said, El Salvador had a balanced agricultural economy, producing grain, fruit and other crops: "But then came the age of coffee and everything changed. . . . The ambition to make money obliged the capitalists to search for greater extensions of land for coffee plants. . . . If a small landholder refused to sell, the rich man, the coffee man, went to the local departmental *Comandante*."[30]

The verdict on the conversion of the country into an export economy dependent on one crop, on the "economic progress" and modernity organized by the Liberal oligarchy, was in.

Notes

[1] The following discussion of social differentiation and "democratization" relies heavily on Guidos Véjar (1980), *passim;* data and interpretation have also been drawn from Menjívar (1980), pp. 17-71; and González (abril-junio 1978), *passim.*

[2] Guidos Véjar (1980), pp. 63-64, 87.

[3] *Ibid.,* p. 79.

[4] *Ibid.,* p. 69.

[5] Durham (1979), pp. 43, 57.

[6] *Ibid.,* p. 36; and Guidos Véjar (1980), pp. 84-85.

[7] Guidos Véjar (1980), p. 87.

[8] Menjívar (1980), p. 49.

[9] Guidos Véjar (1980), p. 100.

[10] *Ibid.,* p. 108.

[11] *Ibid.,* p. 110.

[12] *Ibid.,* pp. 113-124.

[13] *Ibid.,* pp. 118-131.

[14] Menjívar (1980), p. 55.

[15] *Ibid.*

[16] *Ibid.,* pp. 61-71.

[17] Guidos Véjar (1980), p. 135.

[18] *Ibid.*

[19] Durham (1979), p. 43; Anderson (1971), pp. 83-137.

[20] Browning (1971), p. 207.

[21] Durham (1979), p. 43.

[22] Anderson (1971), p. 1.

[23] Andrew Nikiforuk and Ed Struzik, "The Chilling Story of Canada's Role in the Massacre", *The Globe and Mail* (May 11, 1981).

[24] Anderson (1971), pp. 135-136.
[25] *Ibid.*, p. 131.
[26] *Ibid.*, p. 17.
[27] González (abril-junio 1978), p. 595.
[28] Dalton (1977), pp. 192-193.
[29] Menjíbar (1980), p. 55.
[30] As quoted by Anderson (1971), p. 9.

Failure of Modernization and Industrialization Policies 4

uring the Second World War, El Salvador's export economy
began to show signs of revitalization. After the war, and following the overthrow of General Hernández Martínez's regressive
and brutal dictatorship (1931-1944), the emphasis once again became
"modernization". The country's military leaders began to promote the
building of roads, power plants and water supply systems, they began
again the attempt to diversify the country's exports and work towards
industrialization. In all of this they were aided by the high international
price of coffee in the post-war period, which permitted an expansion of
the domestic market and of government revenues. The trend lasted and
by the 1970s the economic and social structures of El Salvador had been
transformed in fundamental ways. Military dictatorships continued to
rule the country (see Table IV), but now as "developmentalists" and
"modernizers" ostensibly oriented towards "moderate reforms" and
even a limited political democratization.

Young economists and *técnicos*, inspired by the development promotion theories of the United Nations Economic Commission for Latin
America (ECLA, or, in its Spanish acronym, CEPAL), entered new and
revamped state agencies that would design policies to overcome the
country's underdevelopment. Unions and political parties were allowed
to organize in the cities, albeit under the surveillance of the government
and subject to periodic repression. Elections were organized and in
1964, for the first time since 1931, opposition representatives occupied
seats in the national legislature.[1] The prohibition on rural organization,
however, remained.

In economic terms, the policies of the "modernizers" were as successful as the coffee oligarchy's had been earlier. Cotton and sugar were
added to the mix of agricultural exports. Roads, together with malaria
and yellow fever control, opened up the coastal lowlands for productive
use. Industry grew spectacularly, reaching a rate of 8.1 per cent per year

43

Table IV
Heads of State — El Salvador (1931-1979)

1931-34	General Maximiliano Hernández Martínez
1934-35	General Andrés Ignacio Menéndez
1935-44	General Maximiliano Hernández Martínez
1944	General Andrés Ignacio Menéndez (ruled for several weeks after a popular uprising toppled Martínez)
1945	Colonel Osmín Aguirre y Salinas
1945-48	*General Salvador Castañeda Castro
1948-50	Military Government Council
1950-56	*Major (later Colonel) Oscar Osorio
1956-60	*Colonel José Maria Lemus
1960-61	Government Revolutionary Junta
1961-62	Civilian-Military Directorate
1962	Dr. Rodolfo F. Cordón (lawyer)
1962-67	*Colonel Julio A. Rivera
1967-72	*Colonel (later General) Fidel Sánchez Hernández
1972-77	Colonel Arturo Armando Molina
1977-79	General Carlos Humberto Romero

Source: Armstrong, "El Salvador — Why Revolution?", NACLA Report, p. 17.

* Military heads of state considered progressive during most or a part of their tenure in office. The coup of 1948 was supposed to lead to a "controlled revolution". Colonel Julio A. Rivera committed his country to the social and economic development aims of the Alliance for Progress.

between 1960 and 1970.[2] Urbanization also accelerated; in 1971, 34 per cent of the population lived in cities of 20,000 or more people, in contrast to 21 per cent in 1931 and 26 per cent in 1950. A prosperous middle class, together with the upper class, made up 13.6 per cent of the population by 1970. As well, an industrial working class, 11.1 per cent of the population in 1970, emerged in the urban centres.[3] And the people who had gained new wealth from industrial and commercial growth were integrated with the coffee oligarchy.

But as before, the social costs of economic success were high. The bulk of the people remained as poor as they had ever been. The distribution of income may have even worsened; the living conditions of up to 75 per cent of the population remained static or deteriorated.

The Diversification of Export Agriculture and Continuing Dispossession of the Peasantry

In the rural areas, a third phase of dispossession was set into motion with "yet another phase of land concentration" stimulated by the diversification of export agriculture.[4]

Cotton production, which had begun to expand slowly in the late 1930s, was further encouraged during the Second World War when the difficulty of importing cotton textiles induced the establishment of a domestic textile industry. Production expanded steadily following the war. Then, after 1958, it skyrocketed on the Pacific coastlands as disease control and the completion of a paved highway, the *Litoral*, made the area commercially attractive. Favourable world market conditions in the 1950s and early 1960s provided further stimulus.

Unfortunately, this expansion of large-scale commercial cotton farming took place in the "one remaining area of fertile coastland into which formerly the dispossessed and landless cultivators of the interior were able to move".[5] Further, the increased acreage planted in cotton took land away from both cattle ranching and subsistence farming, ousting from their land both tenants and squatters. According to Browning: "Though maize and rice, formerly grown on small plots, were often cultivated as an alternative cash-crop on some of the new plantations, and though the total area of cultivable land was increased along the coast by forest clearance, the production of basic food crops in the area increased slowly and in the case of beans, actually decreased."[6]*

Just as important is the fact that cotton plantations are capital-intensive operations. The actual picking of the fibre requires large numbers of labourers, but on a seasonal basis only. The rest of production is generally fully mechanized, requiring only a small, semi-skilled resident workforce.[7] For example, one 15,000-acre plantation studied by David Browning employed a total regular workforce of only thirty-five people.

"In commercial terms," Browning writes, "the colonization of the coastal plain was a success. Ninety percent of the 1964 cotton crop was exported, accounting for twenty-four percent of the country's total exports. The supply of cotton fiber and cotton seed oil has made possible the local manufacture of textiles, margarine and cattle feed."[8] The other side of the picture, however, is the social price paid for this commercial achievement:

> A minority of the coastal population is able to work as resident labourers on the new plantations; the majority is obliged to settle

---

*Agricultural Production Along the Coast, 1950 and 1963

Crop	Production (metric tons)		% Change
	1950	1963	
Cotton Seed	9,321	119,768	+1,223
Cotton Fiber	5,565	71,441	+1,197
Sugar	39,015	63,134	+ 62
Rice	9,453	11,941	+ 26
Maize	130,307	153,246	+ 18
Beans	16,471	14,475	− 12

Source: Browning, *El Salvador: Landscape and Society*, p. 235.

*where it can, to seek whatever form of precarious living it can find,
and has become a poor and dispossessed section of the community.
Moreover, the seasonal nature of the labour requirements of the
cotton plantations has caused the problems of these people to be
neglected; it is considered that any attempt to provide them with a
permanent occupation or income must necessarily reduce the numbers of workers available during the short and critical picking season.*[9]

Along with expansion of cotton growing went sugar production —
another capital-intensive operation. From 10,000 hectares planted
annually in the 1930s, sugarcane production grew to 28,000 hectares in
1971, with exports increasing by almost 1,000 per cent in the same
period.[10] Again, most of this expansion took place on large holdings,
displacing tenant farmers.*

Both land and work were thus denied to the rural population in
order to provide a cheap and plentiful labour force for the seasonal
needs of export agriculture. At the same time the stagnation in food-
crop production coincided with El Salvador's most rapid population
growth. As such, it necessarily induced severe hardship for the rural
population in particular, as well as creating national dependence on
food imports. However, the oligarchy brushed aside the needs and
demands for land of small farmers and tenants, and ignored the urgent
need for expanding rural employment. The subsistence peasants even
had to subsidize the urban economy on the fewer miserable plots that
were left for them: the price of the corn they produced was controlled
for the benefit of the city consumer.

Within this distorted socio-economic structure, even the extension
in 1965 of minimum wage legislation to the rural areas worked to the
disadvantage of agricultural labour. Although these laws were enforced
inconsistently, large estate owners found it advantageous to reduce the
numbers of permanent workers and *colonos* (workers provided with
plots). Moreover, it is not clear to what extent the marginally-improved
wages compensated for the elimination of meals provided by the
employer previous to 1965. Finally, the law resulted in the complete
exclusion of rural women from permanent positions because of their
lower labour productivity.[12] Simultaneously, income derived from
handicraft production traditionally performed by women declined in
the face of competition from urban manufactured goods.[13] The
"Americanization" of cultural values influenced these changes in consumption habits — the artisan products of the rural populations came to
be considered "crude", not modern, and therefore "inferior".[14]

---

* According to Durham, "The expanded production of lesser commercial crops
(tobacco and sesame in particular) has probably also contributed to the increasing concentration of land."[11]

Source: David Browning, *El Salvador: Landscape and Society.*

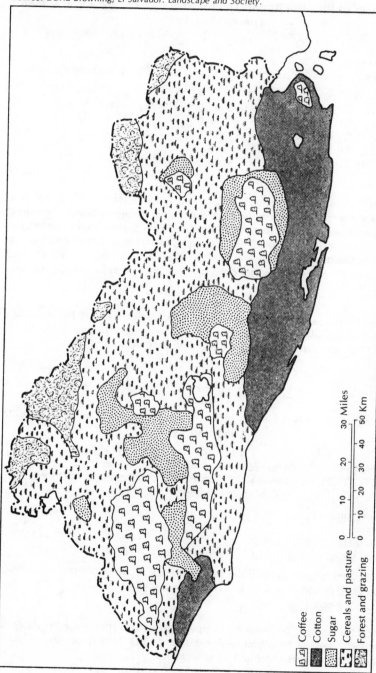

Map 6. Agricultural Regions.

Coffee
Cotton
Sugar
Cereals and pasture
Forest and grazing

0   10   20   30 Miles
0   10   20   30   40   50 Km

Table V*
Changes in the Structure of Land Ownership and the Rural Labour Force (1961-1975)

Categories of Families	1961 No. of Families	%	1971 No. of Families	%	1975 No. of Families	%
Without land	30,451	11.8	112,108	29.1	166,922	40.9
Less than 1 Ha.	107,054	41.6	132,907	34.6	138,838	34.1
From 1 to 1.9 Has.	48,501	18.8	59,842	15.6	62,385	15.3
From 2 to 4.9 Has.	37,743	14.7	44,202	11.4	24,400	6.0
From 5 to 9.9 Has.	14,001	5.5	15,730	4.1	7,545	1.9
More than 10 Has.	19,597	7.6	19,951	5.2	7,297	1.8
Total	257,347	100.0	384,540	100.0	407,387	100.0

* In *El Salvador Land Reform, 1980-81: Impact Audit*, p. 37, Simon and Stephens refer to a work based on PREALC and United Nations data that arrives at the same conclusions summarized in the above table. Note also: for reading this table, it is necessary to know that "nine hectares are the minimum necessary to provide subsistence for a family of six". Also, that in 1971 "more than 60 percent of all holdings were operated by some form of rental or lease arrangement".[15]

Source: Carlos Samaniego, "Movimiento campesino o lucha del proletariado rural en El Salvador?", *Revista Méxicana de Sociología*, p. 661. Data drawn from El Salvador Project 73/003/UNDP and other sources.

Table VI
Average Annual Net Family Income in the Salvadorean Countryside, 1961 and 1975

Category of Family	1961 Average Income (colones)	Calculated in 1975 colones*	1975 Average Income	Difference
Without land	568	940	792	−148
Less than 1 Ha.	756	1,252	1,003	−249
1 to 9.9 Has.	1,058	1,752	2,287	+535
10 to 50 Has.	3,630	6,010	6,342	+332

* Calculated on the basis of the average index of consumer prices in 1975. Information provided by the Central Reserve Bank of El Salvador. The averages include self-consumption.

Source: Samaniego, "Movimiento campesino o lucha del proletariado rural en El Salvador?", *Revista Mexicana de Sociología*, p. 663. Data drawn from El Salvador Project 73/003/UNDP and other sources.

Source: David Browning, *El Salvador: Landscape and Society.*

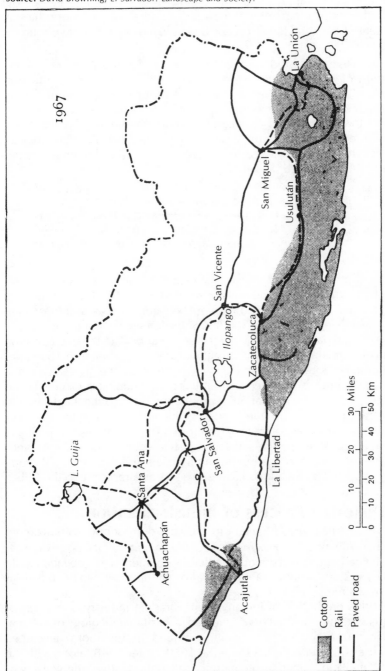

Map 7. The road and rail network. 1940-67.

As Tables V and VI show, the dispossession of the rural population and denial of employment and income are a continuing reality in El Salvador, most eloquently expressed by one statistic: "More than 50 percent of the rural labor force is unemployed more than two-thirds of the year."[16]

Despite very rapid population growth, landlessness and deterioration of rural incomes were not produced simply by "population pressure", as William Durham has cogently demonstrated. They derive, most importantly, from the rural population being denied access to land due to the expansion of commercial export agriculture.[17] While "sixty percent of El Salvador's rural families earn less than the minimum . . . needed to buy subsistence food products",[18] large holdings are not intensively cultivated. In 1961:

> Farms of more than 50 hectares accounted for nearly 60 per cent of El Salvador's total farmland and cultivated less than 35 per cent of this area. In fact, 45.8 per cent of all the land in these farms was used for pasture. Moreover, a full 32 per cent of the land classified as under cultivation on these farms was actually fallow in that year.[19]

In this context, it was hardly surprising that Salvadorean peasant migration to neighbouring Honduras accelerated in the 1950s and 1960s. By 1969, when the Soccer War broke out between the two countries, there may have been as many as 300,000 Salvadoreans in Honduras.

As in the past, so now also in the post-war period, the expropriation of an ever greater segment of the agricultural population from sources of livelihood was carried out in the name of progress: the diversification of the agricultural export economy, aimed at reducing dependence on coffee; and the modernization of production through mechanization to increase productivity. In the 1960s, yet another component was added: the military regimes ruling El Salvador said the country was adhering to the goals of development and social justice enunciated in the Alliance for Progress, the package of reform proposals and economic aid promises presented by the United States in 1961 as a response to the Cuban Revolution.

A Distorted Process of Industrialization

El Salvador had already begun to promote domestic industrialization, another Alliance for Progress favourite, as part of its post-war self-proclaimed efforts to surmount underdevelopment and dependency. In early 1952, for instance, an industrial promotion law had been legislated by decree.

In this promotion of initiatives encouraging industry, a number of mutually reinforcing factors converged. A veritable ideology of national industrialization had been gaining ground in the more developed countries of Latin America since the 1930s; after 1948, along with the idea of Latin America economic integration, this ideology was

The Dynamics of Land Concentration in El Salvador, 1524-1971

The histogram for Phase III allows for 138,031 landless workers in 1971 (21.8 per cent of the agricultural population). **Sources:** Phase I, D. Browning, 1971, Phase II, Asociación Cafetalera de El Salvador 1940, Phase III, ESDGEC 1975, 1977. Durham, *Scarcity and Survival in Central America,* p. 45.

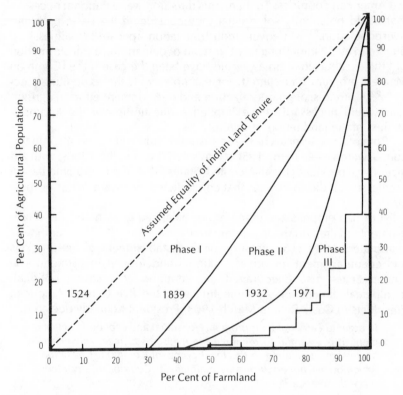

Note: Only two of the phases identified by Durham have been discussed here, and what Durham identifies as Phase II was subdivided into two sequences: the late nineteenth and early twentieth centuries; and the 1920s.

popularized in the region as a whole by the United Nations Economic Commission for Latin America (ECLA), which promoted the idea of a Central American Common Market. Simultaneously, the high prices of El Salvador's coffee exports and the reactivation of the urban economy, which had begun during the War, had resulted in the emergence of a small group of industrialists, as well as commercial and financial sectors controlling investment capital.[20] Finally, ECLA's initiatives towards the organization of a Central American Common Market that would create a viable market for the industrial products of these small countries were particularly well received by El Salvador's now somewhat diversified socio-economic elite, a revitalized or "modernized oligarchy". These select few perceived an industrialization based on a market enlarged by economic integration and the free movement of labour among the Central American countries. To them, this direction was a national necessity that could potentially solve what they considered the basic problem: overpopulation.[21] Moreover, industrialization appeared "painless"; it offered to add "something new" instead of demanding a transformation of "the existing situation as would have been the case if the [Common Market] program had started, for example, with the agricultural sector".[22] A broad-scale modernization and development effort in agriculture would necessarily have implied a questioning of the appropriateness of the land tenure structure.

Both of these approaches — industrialization and economic integration — were visible in the 1950s. However, it was in the 1960s, with aid incentives provided by the United States, that their implementation accelerated. It did so in ways that contradicted the original ECLA proposals.

ECLA had emphasized planning for balanced growth and the establishment of regional or "integration industries".* That emphasis evaporated under U.S. pressure for the establishment of free markets and encouragement for private national and *foreign* investment. The United States also encouraged the adoption of a strong political, ideological dimension. At a meeting with the five Central American Presidents in Costa Rica in March 1963, President Kennedy declared:

> In order to carry out their programs for social and economic betterment, it is essential to reinforce the measures to meet subversive aggression originating in the focal points of Communist agitation which Soviet imperialism may maintain in Cuba or in any other place in America.[24]

Out of this, El Salvador did experience a remarkable industrial expansion. The annual rate of growth in manufacturing averaged 8.1 per cent between 1960 and 1970.[25] The country also diminished its dependence on primary exports: the share of manufactures in total exports increased from 5.6 per cent in 1960 to 17.1 per cent in 1965 and 28.7 per cent in 1970, with most of the goods destined for Central American Common Market countries.[26] The total number of persons employed in industry (including coffee and sugar processing) increased

---

* Regional or integration industries were intended to promote national industrialization for the Central American area as a whole. These industries would have been allocated among the five participating countries so as to assure benefits for all. They would have had the exclusive right to free trade in the Common Market for ten years and would have been selected on the basis of local raw-material endowments.[23]

from 51,738 in 1951 to 85,038 in 1961 and 248,165 in 1971. Nevertheless, the economic and social advances that these statistics suggest, and which government officials were likely to cite, are misleading.

First, almost all the growth took place in the capital city, San Salvador, thereby worsening the disparities in living standards between this centre and the country as a whole. In a book published in 1973, Alastair White points out that "80 per cent of the gross income declared by persons and companies for income tax purposes is reported in the Department of San Salvador".[27]

Second, the new manufacturing enterprises, in fact, generated little employment. Isolating manufacturing proper from industry (which includes sugar and cotton processing), there were approximately 25,000 workers employed in the sector in 1968.[28] While manufacturing had grown at an average annual rate of 8.1 per cent between 1960 and 1970, employment in the sector grew at an annual rate of only 1.8 per cent.[29] Given the capital intensity of the foreign investment* (particularly of U.S.-based transnational corporations) that entered the country in the 1960s under the auspices of the Alliance for Progress, the proportion of industrial workers in the total labour force actually declined from 13.1 per cent in 1960 to 11.1 per cent in 1970.[31]

Third, as the share of foreign investment in the economy increased, so did the amounts of repatriated profits. The Salvadorean state encouraged foreign firms to enter the country by offering special incentives rather than by encouraging companies to respond to domestic needs, such as job creation and local capital accumulation.

Fourth, the use of imported raw materials and intermediate goods in the new industries deepened El Salvador's dependency on foreign powers and exports (which had to provide the funds to pay for the imports).

Fifth, the state revenues and investment capital poured into the industrial and urban sectors could not be used for other purposes, such as programmes to transform subsistence agriculture and food production. Thus, El Salvador became dependent as well on food imports. According to a report from the Inter-American Development Bank, "The leading farm imports in 1972 were wheat, milk, vegetables and fruits, which represented half of the total purchases of goods abroad."[32]

Sixth, further industrial expansion was blocked by the fact that up to 75 per cent of the population lacked the necessary incomes to become

* A number of other factors also contributed to the adoption of capital-intensive techniques. Among them White notes the "aspiration of industrialists" "to create a modern rather than a second-class economy". But it may also be "that industrialists avoid having a large labour force in their factories in order to feel safe from the risk of strikes". Finally, "Most of the training of businessmen and technicians alike is in countries, such as the United States, where the modern, capital-intensive, techniques are more appropriate."[30]

consumers of the goods produced — a dilemma that meant the indus-trial expansion of the 1950s and 1960s could not be sustained in the 1970s. This was compounded by the fact that the Central American Common Market arrangements unravelled following El Salvador's 1969 Soccer War with Honduras. Moreover, the opening of factories may have reduced the incomes of lower class artisans and service workers who competed in the same markets. As White puts it, "The opening of a new factory usually leads people to spend money on its products which would otherwise have been spent in the lower sector, and so causes a further transfer of income out of that sector. In other words, it increases unemployment and depresses incomes."[33]

But even if the Central American Common Market had been con-stituted as originally proposed by ECLA, its workability for sustaining viable industrialization was dubious. That depended on improving the capacity of peasants to consume the products of industry. If this did not happen — and there was no allied policy to see that it would — then, "The creation of a regional market of 15 million people in Central America was an illusion," as Isaac Cohen Orantes puts it.[34] In 1967, the peasantry in Central America accounted for approximately 50 per cent of the regional population, and "for no more than 10-15 percent of monetary circulation".[35]

For all these reasons, El Salvador's industrialization took on dis-torted forms. This supposedly "painless" road of adding to the total economic pie — which paid no attention to the country's fundamental distributional problems — led to greater dependency, failed to generate jobs (perhaps even directly worsened unemployment) and may have led to even greater inequality in the distribution of income. Due to stronger linkages created with the U.S. economy and investors, industrialization also led to the Americanization of El Salvador's urban culture (more and more becoming a consumer culture). As well, it increased the native oligarchy's propensity to invest its profits abroad, thereby further impoverishing the domestic economy.

The Americanization of consumption standards also had direct, and negative, repercussions on the economy of the lower classes. For exam-ple, although corn flour is locally produced, the country began to import wheat flour. According to White, this was all part of moderniza-tion: "The association of wheat bread with high status and [corn] tortil-las with low tends to bias consumption in favor of the imported and industrially processed product and so take more money out of the lower sector."[36] In short, during this contemporary phase of modernization, as in the rural economy, so in the urban economy, the poorest majorities were dispossessed from the sources of a gainful livelihood.

Urban Growth and Union Organization

While Salvadorean industrialization could be considered successful only in the narrowest sense of increased production, the urban sector as a whole did expand: it was there, as usual, that incomes generated in export agriculture and industry were spent. The great proportion of state investment in education, health and services was also concentrated in the cities, particularly in San Salvador. And there, where more and more of the national income was concentrated and generated, modern middle and working classes did develop. As in the 1920s, when similar processes of urban diversification were at work (albeit on a comparatively minor scale), these classes began to organize and demand a democratization of the political system. Once again unions were organized (see Table VII), strikes began to take place, university students formed associations and opposition political parties were founded.

All of these organizations functioned in the shadow and under the limits of the anti-Communism bequeathed to El Salvador from the Peasant Rebellion of 1932. As we've seen, the officially sponsored *matanza* which had followed the rebellion had been conveniently forgotten, but in the official press the violence of the peasantry and the role of the Communist Party in the uprising had been grossly exaggerated. According to these accounts, hundreds of hardworking landowners and leading citizens had been killed by "Communist hordes".

Table VII
Number of Unions and Union Members
El Salvador, 1962-1975

Year	No. of Unions	No. of Members
1962	78	25,917
1963	87	27,734
1964	70	20,922
1965	68	24,475
1966	80	24,126
1967	124	31,214
1968	104	34,573
1969	104	40,717
1970	113	44,150
1971	121	47,020
1972	124	49,886
1973	117	54,387
1974	122	62,999
1975	127	64,186

The Cuban Revolution of 1959, the Latin American guerrilla movements of the 1960s and the "containment of Communism" objectives of the Alliance for Progress strongly reinforced the existing ideological biases. Consequently, signs of militancy or independence on the part of workers quickly provoked repression and counter-measures. A clandes-

tine *Comité de Reorganización Obrero Sindical* (CROSS)* was formed
and enjoyed a brief period of legal existence between 1948 and 1952.[37]
Then, in 1957, a political opening under the government of Colonel
José Maria Lemus (1956-1960) permitted the organization of the *Primer
Congreso Sindical Nacional*.† It in turn led to the foundation of the
Confederación General de Trabajadores de El Salvador (CGTS).** This
time the government responded, with help from the AFL-CIO, by organiz-
ing the competing *Confederación General de Sindicatos de El Salvador*
(CGSS)†† in 1958. With resources available from the government, the
CGSS succeeded in incorporating a large sector of the working class.
Simultaneously, the independent CGTS leadership faced repression and
was forced to work in semi-clandestinity.[38]

In the 1960s, renewed attempts to organize outside government
control took place, this time more successfully. The seven remaining
unions of the CGTS united with a number of independent unions to form
the *Federación Unitaria Sindical de El Salvador* (FUSS)*** in 1965. It
began to recover unions from the government-sponsored confederation,
now reorganized into four federations.††† A National Union of Catholic
Workers**** (later renamed Christian Workers) was organized in 1964.
All this organizational activity coincided with increased strike action.

At the end of the 1960s and the beginning of the 1970s, the urban
working class was manifesting new signs of militancy and independence. Nevertheless, the movement remained divided and comparatively weak. Government control of a large segment of urban labour was
facilitated by the fact that most enterprises were small, thereby permit-
ting the maintenance of paternalistic relationships between worker and
employer. Moreover, workers who had jobs in highly productive,
capital-intensive enterprises could be co-opted through material
rewards. And, to maintain the appearance of democracy within the
contours of the military dictatorship, a measure of labour and welfare

---

* Committee of Worker Union Reorganization. The following discussion of
working class organization relies essentially on Menjíbar (1979).
† First National Union Congress.
** General Confederation of the Workers of El Salvador.
†† General Confederation of Unions of El Salvador.
*** Unitary Union Federation of El Salvador.
††† These were the *Federación de Sindicatos de Trabajadores de Alimentos,
Bebidas y Similares* (FESINTRABS), the *Federación de Sindicatos de Trabajadores
Textiles, Similares y Conexos* (FEXINTEXSIC), the *Federación de Sindicatos de
Trabajadores de la Industria y Servicios Varios* (FESINTRISEVA), and the *Federación
de Sindicatos de la Industria de la Construcción, Similares y Transporte* (FESIN-
CONSTRANS). After 1968 some unions broke away from these official federations.
For example, three unions disaffiliated from FESINTEXSIC and formed the indepen-
dent FENASTRAS in 1972. There were also breakaways from FESINTRISEVA.[39]
**** *Unión Nacional de Obreros Católicos*, later, *de Obreros Cristianos*.

legislation benefitting the working classes was actually implemented —
while their independent leadership faced continued harassment or out-
right repression.

Urban Political Organization and Rural Repression

The restricted but nevertheless real political opening that permitted the
working class to organize in the 1960s formed part of the democratic
image that the ruling military modernizers made an effort to project. As
in the 1920s, the prosperity of the urban economy facilitated this opening, although at the same time the marginal population in the cities —
those people who could not obtain permanent or temporary employment that would generate sufficient income to meet basic needs — was
also growing at an alarming rate. In addition, younger members of the
officer corps who were mildly interested in reform appeared to be gaining ground in the military, while more open-minded members of the
oligarchy (now including industrialists as well as commercial and financial groups) advocated rule through at least partial consensus. After all,
a circumscribed amount of political conflict could bring about those
minor reforms and modifications that could strengthen the system as a
whole, especially if it appeared to be responding to popular demands.
Moreover, they recognized, rule through sheer coercion was always
messy and created international embarrassment.

   Thus, the military guardians of oligarchic privilege also permitted
the organization of opposition political parties, which genuinely contested municipal and national elections in the urban areas. The Christian
Democratic Party, founded in 1960, became the most important of the
opposition organizations in the cities. It and the other parties took
advantage of political privileges that were not extended to the rural
areas, which still formed the economic backbone of El Salvador's
oligarchy and where the majority of the population resided.

   While the secret ballot was, on the whole, respected in the cities, in
the countryside, "When the *campesino* arrives at the polling booth, he
finds persons of authority there, and very likely soldiers or *guardias*
standing around. Finally, the ballot boxes are made of transparent plas-
tic."[40] Even "left-wing proselytization" could be heard in the cities
during election campaigns and during independent union organization
drives. But, "In the rural areas, however, a totally different standard
applies, with what is virtually a separate legal code (the *Ley Agraria*)
and a separate militarized police force (the *Guardia Nacional* as
opposed to the urban *Policía Nacional*) enforce it."[41]

   In this situation, the landowners exercised arbitrary power. Legislation dating from the "Depression dictatorship" of Hernández Martínez
and the aftermath of the *matanza* required National Guardsmen to capture any "suspicious-looking" character "upon the first request of a

hacendado or grower".[42] Indeed, National Guard units, manned by soldiers who made a life-time career in the force, tended to operate as the private armies of local landlords. Agrarian reform and peasant organization were taboo subjects even in urban political circles. Any mention of them immediately raised the spectre of the Peasant Rebellion of 1932 for the oligarchy and was roundly condemned as evidence of Communist subversion. This favoured position has continued to the present: coffee producers are still exempt from paying income taxes; they do pay an export tax but it is not onerous and, since it is not progressive, the small producer is effectively penalized.

For the majority, the modernization policies of the post-World War II period and El Salvador's ostensible commitment to Alliance for Progress reforms yielded no visible benefits. As was his wont, poet Roque Dalton satirized the divorce between the magnitude of the country's problems and the "ant's solutions" proffered by both the government and the well- and not-so-well-meaning military reformers:

> *The present social regime is unjust: let's build latrines.*
> *We are drowning in theft: let's leave used clothing on the door step*
> *So that the good thief won't have to go into the house.*
> *Prostitution is proliferating: let's teach the girls how to read*
> *Exploitation is the principal human relation of the country: let us pray.*[43]

The Militarization of the State

While the National Guard often acted directly on the orders of the landowning oligarchy in the rural areas, the military institution as a whole also increased its own power and privileges vis-à-vis the oligarchy. Since the 1930s, "The army [had] protected the economic interests of the oligarchs and the oligarchs [had] helped the military officers to use government to line their own pockets."[44] Through their governing functions, especially during the post-World War II period of modernization which brought an expansion of the state's role, military officers acquired greater directive powers and even more of a stake in the system. They became the managers and directors of many semi-autonomous state agencies, such as the Central Reserve Bank, the Salvadorean Social Security Institute, the national airline and the census bureau.[45] A kind of co-government of the military *with* rather than simply *for* the oligarchy emerged in the 1950s and 1960s, and fortified itself in the 1970s.

Consequently, the motivations for embarking on a military career had little to do with professional achievement or with serving the nation.

> *Young men enter the officer corps to acquire the power and the spoils military service provides.... Each officer comes from a graduating class, called a* tanda, *and each* tanda *has a president.*
> *Loyalty to the* tanda *is generally greater and more commanding*

than loyalty to the institution in which they serve. During their thirty year careers, the officers of a tanda *seek contacts, form alliances with other* tandas *and otherwise prepare for their goal of political power.*

Every five years, in the past, elections were held. No matter which party had the most ballots, the army won. Together they assembled a coalition of officers from one major tanda *and several allied* tandas *which were to enjoy the spoils of office for the next five years.*[46]

The military thus became a caste which thrived on the opportunities for corruption and economic advancement provided through its near-monopoly of the highest political offices. While American military aid and training programmes in the 1960s (see Appendix II) gave a more professional veneer to the Salvadorean military, they did nothing to counteract these corrupt practices.* Rather, the American emphasis on counter-insurgency fortified the Salvadorean officers' most reactionary habits, particularly their identification of popular demands for reform with Communist subversion.

While the system of military/oligarchic domination remained intact, the socio-economic transformation of the 1950s and 1960s combined with the restricted urban political opening of the latter decade, set the stage for an increasing political awareness that, as in the 1920s, spilled over to the rural areas. The repercussions of the 1969 Soccer War and the 1972 presidential elections brought the system to the current crisis, which saw more than 2,000 Salvadoreans die per month in 1980 and 1981.

* In addition to providing military assistance to the Central American countries, the United States prompted the organization of the Central American Defense Council (CONDECA) in 1964. CONDECA was created to promote cooperation and institutionalized channels of mutual support among the national military institutions of the Central Amercian countries.

Notes

[1] Anderson (1967), pp. 260-266; also, Armstrong (1980), pp. 8-17.
[2] CEPAL (December 1976).
[3] CEPAL (December 1980), pp. 18, 22.
[4] Durham (1979), p. 44.
[5] Browning (1971), p. 225.
[6] *Ibid.,* p. 235.
[7] *Ibid.,* p. 236.
[8] *Ibid.,* p. 239.
[9] *Ibid.*
[10] Durham (1979), p. 44.
[11] *Ibid.*

[12] White (1973), pp. 118-119.
[13] *Ibid.*, p. 140.
[14] *Ibid.*, pp. 143, 173-174.
[15] Simon and Stephens (1981), p. 8.
[16] *Ibid.*, pp. 2, 6.
[17] Durham (1979), pp. 45, 47.
[18] Simon and Stephens (1981), p. 8.
[19] Durham (1979), p. 51.
[20] Menjíbar (1980), pp. 84-86.
[21] Cohen Orantes (1972), p. 10.
[22] *Ibid.*, p. 20.
[23] *Ibid.*
[24] Cited in *Ibid.*, p. 38.
[25] CEPAL (1980), p. 70.
[26] *Ibid.*, p. 94.
[27] White (1973), p. 152.
[28] *Ibid.*, p. 151.
[29] CEPAL (1980), p. 18.
[30] White (1973), p. 227.
[31] CEPAL (1980), p. 18.
[32] IADB (1973), p. 207.
[33] White (1973), pp. 224-225.
[34] Cohen Orantes (1972), p. 86.
[35] Cited in *Ibid.*, p. 44.
[36] *Ibid.*, p. 225.
[37] Menjíbar (1979), pp. 91-92.
[38] *Ibid.*, pp. 92-93.
[39] *Ibid.*, pp. 99-100.
[40] White (1973), p. 209.
[41] *Ibid.*, p. 208.
[42] Cited by Webre (1979), p. 21.
[43] Dalton (1977), p. 109.
[44] Gómez in Subcommittee (1981), p. 193.
[45] Sol (1980), p. 44.
[46] Gómez in Subcommittee (1981), p. 194.

A "Soccer War" and a Presidential Election 5

On July 14, 1969, the Salvadorean army invaded Honduras after a series of border clashes following the forceful expulsion of Salvadoreans from the neighbouring country. Earlier in June, in an effort to stop the expulsions, El Salvador had filed a complaint of "genocide" before the Inter-American Human Rights Commission against Honduras, which had absorbed large numbers of Salvadorean migrants since the 1920s.

The war lasted only four days. Under pressure from the United States and the Organization of American States, El Salvador agreed to a cease-fire on July 18. In the following months, some 130,000 of the estimated 300,000 Salvadoreans resident in Honduras returned home as refugees.[1]

Foreign journalists labelled the conflict the "Soccer War" because it broke out "just after three hotly contested soccer games in the qualifying rounds for the 1969 World Cup".[2] In a more serious vein, the conflict was also dubbed a "population war". It was argued that El Salvador, which still has one of the highest population growth-rates in the world, had found a demographic "safety valve" in less densely-populated Honduras.* The cause of the war was thus ascribed, as have been other of the country's problems, to over-population. Searching for specific sources of hostility between the two countries in the economic sphere, some analysts pointed to El Salvador's favourable balance of trade with Honduras and to the retardation of Honduran industrial development due to the competition of Salvadorean manufactured goods imported under Common Market agreements.

The fundamental and less visible sources of the conflict, however, lay in the land-concentrating policies of the agricultural oligarchies of

---

* El Salvador is among the most densely populated of the Latin American countries, with 8,260 square miles of land and 4.6 million people in 1980.

61

both countries. Honduran landowners, faced with a militant peasant movement demanding land reform, found a scapegoat in the Salvadorean settlers. In turn, the Salvadorean oligarchy feared that a refugee influx would increase pressure for land reform within its own borders, "easily the most sensitive and dangerous [of the country's] political issues".[3] Like so many other events in El Salvador's history, the "Soccer War" was not what its name suggested. Arising as it did out of land concentration on both sides of the border, it might more appropriately be called the "Landlords' War".

Officially, the Salvadorean government justified its invasion by arguing that human rights were "not negotiable".[4] But the real fears of the country's ruling oligarchy were perhaps more accurately, if irreverently, portrayed by poet Roque Dalton:

> We're indifferent about land reform as long as it takes place in another country. But I don't see why we should pay for the broken plates of the Honduran agrarian reform. If General López Arellano [President of Honduras] wants to engage in Communist demagoguery, he should do it without annoying his neighbors. If the 350 thousand Salvadoreans who live by working hard in Honduras come back to our country, unemployment will be multiplied by 350 thousand and the national situation would reach the edge of revolution. And that has to be avoided. One way or another.[5]

Causes of the Soccer War: Peasant-Landlord Conflict in Honduras

The step-by-step expropriation of the Salvadorean peasantry provoked by the expansion and, later, the mechanization of export agriculture has been discussed extensively in the previous chapters. Suffice to reiterate that peasant migration to Honduras stemmed from these forces and the resultant pressure on land, a situation created by El Salvador's agricultural oligarchy.

In Honduras, for a variety of historical reasons that will not be examined here, the first generalized phase of agricultural modernization became noticeable only in the 1950s and 1960s.* Up to that time, the Honduran countryside was characterized by a variety of non-property forms of tenure: the peasantry continued to cultivate ejidal, public and untitled lands. In addition, peasants could rent land on traditional estates through a variety of tenancy arrangements.[6] With the expansion of

* Banana production was concentrated in a previously sparsely populated area and formed a modern "enclave" in an otherwise traditional agricultural economy. An "enclave" may be defined as a region (specializing in a particular type of export production) that is relatively isolated from the domestic economy of the country where the investment for export production originates. In the case of Honduran banana production, the foreign corporation involved was the U.S.-based United Fruit Company.

the national road network in the 1950s and 1960s, landowners started to modernize their estates. Commercial cotton and cattle production expanded, and the consequences for peasant access to land were identical to those encountered earlier in El Salvador:

> Large areas of ejidal and national land [were] incorporated by the systematic extension of hacienda boundaries [usually for the price of barbed-wire fencing], usurping in this manner the rights of ejidal land using peasants with titles dating back many years. . . . This process was repeated in "community after community" . . . becoming known as the Enclosure Movement.[7]

As land values increased, landowners also found it profitable to eliminate tenancy relationships. Both the mechanization of cotton production and large-scale cattle ranching implied a reduction of the agricultural labour force needed on the estates. Finally, the United Fruit Company released 19,000 workers in the 1950s from its banana plantations on the north coast of Honduras.[8]

These transformations affected the Salvadorean immigrants as much as the native Honduran peasantry. Up to 30 per cent of the banana workers may have been immigrants. According to various estimates, Salvadoreans made up anywhere from 14.9 to 19.8 per cent of the agricultural labour force of Honduras in 1969.

In strong contrast to the situation in El Salvador, the rural population in Honduras — the natives and immigrants together — organized to resist landlord encroachments. In 1954, a prolonged and well-organized strike had paralyzed production on the United Fruit banana plantations. The strike ultimately led to the legal recognition of the union and to labour legislation for a workforce which numbered 16,000 in the 1960s.[9] A "national campesino movement" emerged after the strike and by the late 1960s, three peasant leagues had been established. With the support of these peasant organizations, "Campesino reclamations [or land invasions as they were often termed in the press] became increasingly frequent in the years before the conflict with El Salvador."[10] The Honduran government had also enacted an Agrarian Reform Law in the early 1960s and upheld peasant claims frequently enough to disconcert large landowners.

In response to peasant pressure, in 1966, the landowners organized themselves into the National Federation of Agriculturalists and Cattle Ranchers of Honduras (FENAGH). FENAGH protested the peasant "land invasions" and in a Federation petition to the government Salvadorean immigrants were "first singled out . . . as principals in the invasions".[11] Wide publicity was given to the landowners' charges that most "land invasions" were conducted by "foreigners". In short, the large numbers of Salvadoreans working in agriculture both threatened the landholdings of the hacendados and added to the pressure for agrarian reform in Honduras:

> To the large landowners, [Salvadoreans] then became a convenient
> scapegoat. Their expulsion offered a means of reducing the threat of
> land occupations and agrarian reform. . . . [By] presenting the con-
> flict in terms of nationality, they obtained a polarization of public
> opinion [at least in the cities] in favour of their interests.[12]

During his field work in the Honduran countryside, William Durham
found no hostility among Honduran peasants toward the Salvadoreans.
On the contrary, all the evidence pointed to cooperation in a joint
struggle against the large landowners. The "Soccer War" truly was the
"Landlords' War".

---

*The monologue of an Honduran planner who is both progressive
and clever:*
"To carry out the Agrarian Reform that the Alliance for Progress
demands from us, we have to redistribute some lands. The problem
is whose lands should be redistributed. It's tabu to touch the lands
of the American United Fruit Company. If we touch the lands of the
big landowning oligarchy of Honduras, the Agrarian Reform would
be Communist. To begin cutting down national forest would be
very expensive. So there's nothing left but the lands cultivated by
the Salvadorean immigrants which come to 370 thousand hectares.
If we expropriate the guanacos,* we'll demonstrate our patriotic
sincerity because we'll be recovering lands in the hands of foreigners for Hondurans. But isn't the United Fruit also foreign, owned as
it is by Yankees? That's beside the point. It is a simple arithmetic
problem because the Salvadoreans who threaten the territorial
integrity of Honduras by residing here are 300 thousand, while the
Yankee residents are no more than three thousand and they are
helping us to civilize ourselves. What's more, our patriotic spirit
will stand out. We'll be like the Yankee agrarian reformers by redis-
tributing lands that they took away from the Indians. And finally, to
demonstrate that we are radicals, we'll decree the expropriation of
the Salvadoreans without any kind of compensation."†

    The expulsion of the Salvadoreans certainly reduced pressure on the
land in Honduras, but the conflict between peasants and landed oligarchy has continued to the present time. In El Salvador, the return of
politicized agricultural labourers, with their organizational experiences
in unions and peasant leagues, added fuel to the already explosive mix
of Salvadorean society.[13]

Conditions in El Salvador When the Refugees Returned

The great majority of Salvadoreans in Honduras had been engaged in
agricultural occupations, as farm labourers, squatters, tenants or small

---

* *Guanaco* is a term popularly used in Central America for Salvadoreans.
† From: Roque Dalton, *Historias Prohibidas del Pulgarcito,* p. 214.

proprietors. Now, jobless and landless, the refugees returned to a homeland where 58.3 per cent of the agricultural labour force, which in turn
made up 60 per cent of the population, was either unemployed or
underemployed.[14] They returned to a country where, even in 1950,
before land concentration had reached its contemporary dimensions,
1.9 per cent of the population owned 57.5 per cent of the land.[15] Only
15 per cent of the country's school teachers served in the rural areas,
where most of the country's 40 per cent-illiterate population lived. With
60 per cent of rural families earning less than the minimum necessary to
buy subsistence foods,[16] malnutrition among children stood at shocking
levels. Between 1971-1975, among children under five, 48.5 per cent
were estimated as suffering from mild malnutrition (in other words,
requiring more and better food for recovery), 22.9 per cent from moderate malnutrition (needing medical attention) and 3.1 per cent from
severe malnutrition (requiring hospitalization for recovery).[17] Most of
these children were rural. But 67 per cent of the country's doctors
worked in San Salvador.

The situation was better in the urban areas and particularly in the
capital city where the bulk of the country's middle class and
permanently-employed working class lived. But even there, the social
crisis was reaching acute proportions as migrants from the countryside
crowded into the shantytowns surrounding San Salvador in search of
non-existent work opportunities. As an Organization of American States
(OAS) publication reports:

> Industrial development based on import substitutions has not led to
> increased employment opportunities at the rates expected. . . .
> [Similarly,] although accompanied by high levels of investment, the
> extension of basic services — electricity, gas, water, transportation
> and communications [also concentrated in the urban sector] — has
> opened up only a small number of jobs.[18]

Most migrants from the rural areas were thus faced with no alternative
but to join the already mushrooming ranks of street vendors, shoeshine
boys, car washers — anything to make a few cents to buy food.

The social costs of the "painless" road to economic development, of
adding to the pie through industrialization and urban infrastructural
projects, had been high indeed. The creation of the Central American
Common Market with its somewhat expanded consumer demand and
free circulation of labour had alleviated some of the pressure on
employment in El Salvador. But with the outbreak of the "Soccer War",
the additional market provided to the country's industries by Honduras'
also small middle and permanently employed working classes was cut
off, as were the possibilities of further labour migration. The value of
manufactured goods in total exports dropped from 28.7 per cent in
1970 to 23.6 per cent in 1975.[19] And the Common Market and the
stability of oligarchic domination in El Salvador were to be the most
prominent casualties of the war. The country was now forced to confront its domestic problems related to land distribution and the addi-

tional economic problems created by the hostilities. Moreover, it had to do so in a climate of heightened political activity and conflict. The political opposition which had emerged in the 1960s was preparing to contest the 1972 Presidential election.

The refugee influx, in effect, broke the taboo on the discussion of agrarian reform in El Salvador. On August 14, 1969, within a month from the outbreak of the War, General Sánchez-Hernández (1967-1972) announced a package of reforms to respond to the crisis. The centre-piece was a rather vague "democratic program of agrarian reform" which would "focus upon the problem in its totality . . . [and be] orien-ted in an integral manner toward a more just distribution of land and greater agricultural productivity".[20]

The government's announcement opened the gate for opposition proposals and pressure. By the end of the month, the Christian Democratic Party (PDC) had presented an alternative of its own. It emphasized the need for a reorganization of the agrarian sector on the basis of "communitarian" consciousness. In effect, however, the PDC posited the creation of "a class of small and medium sized independent farm-ers" who would "serve as the constituency for a vigorous democ-racy".[21]

Proposals of this type by the country's major and rather moderate opposition party, however, were not taken lightly by the landed oligar-chy and their urban business partners in commerce and industry.

The Emergence of a Reformist Opposition: The Christian Democratic Party

The Christian Democratic Party (PDC) had been founded in 1960 by well-to-do and middle class urban professionals.[22] The party, inspired by the principles of social Christianity, was also anti-Communist. This bent gave it a certain legitimacy and during its early years, attracted conservatives disaffected by the arbitrary violence of the military-dominated ruling party, with some hyperbole called the Revolutionary Party of Democratic Unification (PRUD).* The development of the PDC into a "relatively well organized and ideologically coherent" institution with a broadly-based popular following was eased by Col. Julio Rivera's (1962-1967) decision to organize relatively free Legislative Assembly and municipal elections in 1964.[23] By then, the ruling party had been reorganized and renamed as the Party of National Conciliation (PCN).†

The prosperity and general expansion of the urban economy along with government spending on such things as schools and sanitation in the 1960s made Rivera and the PCN secure of their capacity to retain power against any electoral challenge. The PCN, like its predecessor, the PRUD, was steadfastly controlled by the President, known as the party's "General Coordinator". His closest associates and supporters in the

* *Partido Revolucionario de Unificación Democrática.*
† *Partido de Conciliación Nacional.*

party came from his fellow army officers. The next level down in the party structure allowed entry by "a number of civilians, particularly from the professional classes in the capital. It might be described as a kind of labour exchange."[24] In other words, the party provided opportunities for personal advancement and dispensed patronage in the form of jobs and other material benefits.

In addition to its linkages with the "modernized oligarchy", the PCN thus had connections with larger segments of the population. In this respect, it had taken some efforts to imitate Mexico's ruling Institutional Revolutionary Party (PRI)* without achieving the latter's organizational capacity and coherence. Nevertheless, the lower levels of the PCN were composed of "manual workers, peasants and some clerical workers who [had] long-standing connections with the army or some part of the administrative apparatus or both, as well as with the official party".[25] What this did was establish an organized network of clienteles who owed personal allegiance to military and civilian strongmen — a party network which has continued to exist and dispense patronage into the 1980s. The elections proposed for 1982 and 1983 — in the midst of a civil war — by the junta that came to power in 1979 would presumably be contested by this party.

The Christian Democrats attacked the PCN's political hegemony in the 1964 elections with a programme "reminiscent of Alberto Masferrer's Minimum Vital" of the 1920s.[26] They argued for "a revolution in liberty" — neither communist nor capitalist but, rather, a third autonomous path to development, one which would be scientifically and technically planned, in accord with Christian ethics, to ensure social justice and provide a decent living standard for all Salvadoreans. During its early years the party barely addressed agrarian reform. Rather, its leaders reiterated their respect for private property, arguing that "The solution of El Salvador's social problems did not lie in pulling down the oligarchy, but in pulling up the oppressed."[27] Even these moderate proposals, however, were branded as Communism in disguise by various PCN leaders, particularly in the rural areas where "the campesino often regarded his vote as simply part of the tribute owed his patrón".[28]

To their own and the PCN's surprise, the Christian Democrats did well in the 1964 elections — the first authentically contested in thirty years. They won thirty-seven municipalities and fourteen seats in the Legislative Assembly. José Napoleón Duarte, already a prominent PDC leader, emerged victorious in the mayoralty contest in San Salvador. As a reform mayor, he pushed for a rather mild municipal tax reform. In doing so, he confronted the successful opposition of the National Private Enterprise Association (ANEP).† Duarte was more successful in implementing measures that did not touch the pocketbook of the rich:

* Partido Revolucionario Institucional.
† Asociación Nacional de Empresa Privada.

computerizing city record-keeping procedures, improving some services and obtaining an Inter-American Development Bank loan for the construction of two new central markets.[29] The programme that probably had the greatest long-run political impact, however, was Communitarian Action. This venture, initially opposed by the Ministry of the Interior, provided organizational experience for some of the poorest sectors of the urban population. Through its neighbourhood community groups were organized to help build schools, bridges, retaining walls, community centres, parks and gardens, and to participate in other civic projects. The groups, which eventually numbered between sixty and eighty, could work either with the municipality or on their own initiative in solving the city's problems. Communitarian Action, according to Stephen Webre, "was a natural extension of the value the PDC placed on the decentralization of authority and responsibility as well as the encouragement of 'communitarian' as opposed to individualistic values".[30]

The political space for opposition established in 1964 was maintained and even enlarged in the following years. Several small political parties to the left of the PDC, always accused of being Communist, continued to be intermittently repressed and ruled illegal. Nevertheless, the 1967 presidential campaign was relatively open. It was won, as expected, by the official candidate of the PCN, Colonel Sánchez-Hernández (1967-1972). But then, in the 1968 municipal and Legislative Assembly elections, Duarte was re-elected mayor of San Salvador and the Christian Democrats won nineteen seats to the Assembly while other smaller opposition parties gained six: "The opposition now controlled 25 seats to the government's 27."[31] Since the electoral system had been allowed to function since 1964 on the implicit understanding that there would be no actual transfer of power to the opposition, the 1968 elections pointed to a future crisis.

The war with Honduras took place within this crisis in the making, and initially led to the opposition rallying behind the national cause. However, the character of political debate changed dramatically as the influx of 130,000 refugees forced serious discussion of agrarian reform.

A National Debate on Agrarian Reform

The War with Honduras and the subsequent government announcement of August 14, 1969 that it intended to implement an agrarian reform programme followed upon the opposition's 1968 election victories. The government was certainly trying to obtain support for itself. However, the Legislative Assembly now took the initiative and, in an amazing show of its own independence, convoked a National Agrarian Reform Congress to meet in San Salvador January 5-10, 1970. Representation to the Congress, designed to canvass opinion from all sectors of Salvadorean society, was drawn from four sectors: government, nongovernment, labour and private (or entrepreneurial). In his book on Duarte, Stephen Webre argues that the Congress may well have been the most broadly representative political gathering in Salvadorean history, as it represented virtually every political position and economic interest. Excluded, however, were the Salvadorean peasantry and the rural labour force — the people who would be most affected by agrarian reform. Labour delegates quickly criticized this serious omission and were supported in their objections by the *Movimiento Revolucionario Nacional's* Guillermo Ungo.* Nonetheless, labour organizations and members of the left participated willingly and enthusiastically in the Congress and generally considered it a major step forward.[32] But when the Congress empowered itself to make recommendations to the government, all the private sector representatives walked out, in a clear manifestation of their resistance to change. In addition to passing resolutions on technical issues, rural credit, market expansion and more, the Congress proceeded to conclude that the state had a "duty" to undertake "massive expropriation in favour of the common good". It also underlined the need for the organization of rural labour to participate in the implementation of an agrarian reform.

The Christian Democrats and other smaller progressive opposition parties adopted the radical resolutions of the Congress as their own. Thus, the many national institutions represented in the Congress, together with the opposition political parties that would contest the 1972 Presidential election, called on the state to reverse the hundred-year-long process of landlord expropriation of peasant lands.

At the same time that agrarian reform was being placed on the agenda of national debate and possibly, action, members of the urban labour movement were challenging the government-controlled union and federation leadership. Particularly prominent were strikes conducted by the National Association of Salvadorean Educators (ANDES)† in 1968 and 1971. A number of radical student groups had also emerged at the National University, where the student population had quadrupled in the 1960s when admission procedures were democratized to test achievement rather than social connections. But, while the radicalized sectors of the organized labour movement and the university student body could be expected to provide enthusiastic support for agrarian reform, the Church's championship of the cause was more remarkable.

The Transformation of the Catholic Church

As late as 1960, the Catholic Church had organized the trucking of

---

* The head of the present FDR/FMLN opposition alliance; the *Movimiento Revolucionario Nacional* (MNR), founded in 1965, is a social democratic party.
† *Asociación Nacional de Educadores Salvadoreños.*

20,000 peasants to San Salvador to attend a demonstration of support for Colonel José Lemus (1956-1960), at a time when the head of state was confronted with popular opposition in the midst of an economic slump. Archbishop Luís Chávez y González, who by the 1970s advocated agrarian reform and defended peasant rights, had performed the mass that concluded the 1960 demonstration.[33] Earlier, the Church had helped to subdue the 1932 Peasant Rebellion; as a result, "Catholic orthodoxy was converted into a symbol of national loyalty."[34] The *Caballeros de Cristo Rey,* or Knights of Christ the King, organized by priests in the rural areas, had propagated a virulent anti-Communist and militantly conservative ideology.[35] As recently as 1967, the rest of the Church hierarchy had not protested when Archbishop Aparicio threatened to excommunicate the entire leadership of a small opposition party.* The party's crime was that it had dared to propose an agrarian reform during the year's Presidential election campaign.

A transformation, nevertheless, had been coming about during the 1960s in conjunction with the radicalization of Catholic clergy throughout most of Latin America in the same decade. The extreme oppressiveness and inequity of Salvadorean society, the incredible impoverishment of the great majority of the population, particularly in the rural sector, could no longer be rationalized by a clergy that was in touch with new currents of thought in the Church the world over. Thus one of the ideological pillars of the old order joined the call for a profound transformation of the country's socio-economic structure. The development was to have momentous consequences in the 1970s.

The Electoral Fraud of 1972 and the Foundation of ORDEN

By the early 1970s, from the perspective of the country's oligarchy, the political process had run amuck. Unions were organizing strikes, students were demonstrating, opposition political parties were actually winning elections, the Church was defending the rights of peasants to organize themselves, and all of these groups were demanding agrarian reform. For the oligarchy, the political opening had gone too far.

In this climate of tension — aggravated further by increasing violence and government accusations of the PDC's "Communist" tendencies — the 1972 Presidential election took place. To contest the election, the social democratic National Revolutionary Movement (MNR), the progressive Nationalist Democratic Union (UDN)† and the Christian Democrats had formed a coalition, the National Opposition Union

---

* The *Partido Acció Renovadora,* whose presidential candidate was Fabio Castillo, now a member of the FDR/FMLN Alliance. The party was declared illegal after its rallies began to attract large numbers of peasants.

† *Unión Democrática Nationalista.*

(UNO).* And by all objective accounts the election, held on February 20, was won by José Napoleón Duarte, the UNO's presidential candidate, campaigning on a platform pushing for reform. But the government had its own system of calculation and declared its own choice, PCN candidate Colonel Arturo Armando Molina, as new President.

The announcement of Molina's "victory" was followed, in late March, by an attempted coup. Duarte threw in his support for the coup only after military maneuvers had already begun. The coup failed, repression was unleashed against the Christian Democratic Party,[36] and the opening of the political process had come to an end.

Members of the military and landlord class had been suspicious of the process from its inception. Under the leadership of National Guard Director General José Alberto Medrano, they had organized the Democratic Nationalist Organization (ORDEN)† in "semi-secrecy", probably between 1961 and 1965; it was certainly in existence by 1968.[37] ORDEN was established and has continued to operate as "a paramilitary civilian vigilance association composed of many thousand armed peasants with the ostensible mission of combatting communism and defending 'democratic' values in the republic's rural areas".[38] The National Guard, which had traditionally functioned as the private army of the landowners, provided counter-guerrilla military training to ORDEN members, many of them army reservists. The clientelistic networks established between army officers and recruits, and the paternalistic ties which still existed between landlords and some of the rural poor, were utilized to form an extensive vigilante organization — even before there had been any known guerrilla threat or peasant political organization in the country. An effort was made to establish units in all the villages of El Salvador. For those who joined it, ORDEN provided some material security through landlord and military protection and favours.

The establishment of ORDEN, coinciding as it did with the political opening of the mid-1960s, clearly indicated that the oligarchy was never prepared to accept the logical outcome of a democratization of the political process, that is, the political victory of the reformist opposition at the polls. But, while repression increased, a façade of reform and political democracy was maintained for a time after the electoral fraud of 1972. Thus Colonel Molina (1972-77) gave the rather grandiose title of "National Transformation" to his regime. So-called elections were also held. In the last of them, Molina's Defense Minister Carlos Humberto Romero, a counter-insurgency specialist, rose to the presidency in 1977.

* *Unión Nacional Opositora.*
† *Organización Democrática Nacionalista.* ORDEN means "order".

Notes

[1] Durham (1979), p. 170.

[2] *Ibid.* The following interpretation of the "Soccer War" relies essentially on Durham's meticulously-researched work.

[3] Webre (1979), p. 113.

[4] *Ibid.*

[5] Dalton (1977), p. 216; see also: Woodward (1976), pp. 252-255: "Land-owners in El Salvador, fearing a return of the emigrés to El Salvador, where they would demand land, urged Salvadorean President Fidel Sánchez-Hernández to fight on."

[6] Durham (1979), p. 122.

[7] *Ibid.,* pp. 122-123.

[8] *Ibid.,* p. 124.

[9] González (1978), p. 563.

[10] Durham (1979), p. 160.

[11] *Ibid.,* p. 161.

[12] *Ibid.,* p. 165.

[13] Gordon (1980), pp. 208-209.

[14] Soto (1979), pp. 49-50.

[15] Torres Rivas (1969), p. 191; from data compiled by *Comité Interamericano de Dessarrollo Agrícola* (CIDA) of the Organization of American States.

[16] Simon and Stephens (1981), p. 8.

[17] IDB (1978), p. 138.

[18] Soto (1979), p. 40.

[19] CEPAL (1980), p. 94.

[20] Webre (1979), p. 122.

[21] *Ibid.,* p. 124.

[22] The following discussion of the Christian Democratic Party and the political process leading to the 1972 Presidential election relies heavily on Webre.

[23] *Ibid.,* p. 48.

[24] White (1973), p. 193.

[25] *Ibid.,* p. 194.

[26] Webre (1979), p. 59.

[27] *Ibid.,* p. 63.

[28] *Ibid.,* p. 168.

[29] *Ibid.,* pp. 81-88.

[30] *Ibid.,* p. 89.

[31] *Ibid.,* p. 102.

[32] *Ibid.,* p. 126.

[33] *Ibid.,* pp. 28, 130.

[34] Guidos Véjar (1980), p. 137.

[35] Menjívar (1980), p. 40.

[36] Webre (1979), pp. 163-183; Buckley (1981), pp. 41-42, 46-49.

[37] White (1973) p. 207; Arnson (1980), p. 6.

[38] Webre (1979), p. 162.

Crisis and
Revolution   6

A s long as the electoral process appeared viable, the small
groups which began to argue in 1970 that there was no alternative but a "popular war" — that is, organizing an army of the
poor to fight the military organizations of the rich — found a small
audience.* After 1972, the audience began to grow as the moderate
Christian Democratic Party "became the principal target of government
repression" precisely because of its broadly-based popular following.
That backlash "destroyed the party's effectiveness as an electoral opposition, and with it the viability of electoral opposition *per se*".[1] In the
months following the elections and the coup attempt, most PDC leaders
were forced into exile by the repression unleashed by the Molina
regime. José Napoleón Duarte, for example, has described his own
arrest and torture:

> They took me to the central police headquarters with my hands
> handcuffed behind me. I was blindfolded, and my mouth was cov-
> ered with adhesive tape. They left me in the car for a while, and
> then they came back, one by one, no one saying a word, and began
> to beat me. They used their fists, blackjacks, brass knuckles, a pistol
> butt. I could feel the shape of whatever they were beating me with.
> They beat me unconscious in complete silence. Then they dragged
> me, still blindfolded, to a cell. When I came to, they began ques-
> tioning me. They wanted to know how we got the money for the
> campaign. Was it supplied by the Communists? Because they had
> spent millions, they thought we had spent millions. I thought in the
> end they would kill me, but they threw me in a plane and flew me
> to Guatemala.[2]

In the years after 1972, the Christian Democratic rank and file joined
new popular organizations associated with three different revolutionary
armed forces. The Catholic Church also took up the challenge of repre-

* See Appendix II.

73

senting popular interests as the electoral political parties were prevented from functioning. Moreover, the focus of political conflict shifted from the cities to the countryside. For the first time since the massive repression of 1932, the rural population began to organize under the aegis of the radicalized clergy and the revolutionary armed forces.

The Social Action Programmes of the Catholic Clergy and the Escalation of Repression

The leadership provided by Catholic clergy to the peasantry of the sugar-growing region around Aguilares in the Department of San Salvador exemplifies a process repeated in many rural districts during the 1970s. In that area the land tenure structure and the conditions of unemployment and misery were typical of the national situation. Peasants cultivated beans and corn on barren hillside plots and rented parcels of valley land from the sugar plantations at increasing fees. Land values were climbing in tandem with the expansion of sugar production, which provided a significant amount of employment only during the four-month harvest season.

In August 1972 four Jesuits led by Father Rutilio Grande arrived in this sugar-producing region and began to organize non-partisan Christian communities in Aguilares, Paisnal (a neighbouring town) and twenty-eight nearby villages. Sharing the day-to-day life of the poverty-stricken rural population, they succeeded, among other things, in establishing unions. As a result, the local peasantry "began to demand better wages, agrarian reform, and lower prices for seed and fertilizer".[3] These peasants joined the recently-formed Christian Federation of Salvadorean Peasants (FECCAS),* technically illegal because of the explicit legal prohibitions against rural political organization dating from the 1920s. The Jesuits, however, argued that the right to association was guaranteed in the Constitution.

The ideological message of the Jesuits was purely Christian, and they explained their organizational activities with reference to the *New Testament:*

> *The peasants began to open their ears to the "Good News"[which is what the word "Gospel" means] that God is the Father of all people, that all people are brothers and sisters, and that they must not live in conditions of such tremendous inequality that the very Fatherhood of God is denied. At the same time they receive the message that the goodness of God does not make man any less responsible for building a more just world. That is why Jesus called us the "salt of the earth" and the "leaven in the meal".*[4]

The Jesuits worked with the support of "village lay leaders known as 'Delegates of the Word'" and were joined by students who organized literacy programmes.

* *Federación de Campesinos Cristianos de El Salvador.*

Not surprisingly, these activities quickly provoked the strong opposition of landowners who accused the Catholic Church of "instigating class warfare". Despite the accusations, the Jesuits continued their work. Finally, four years later in December 1976, a peasant demonstration organized by FECCAS led to violence. In the demonstration, held to protest the flooding of peasant plots by a hydroelectric project, an estate owner was shot to death. The landowners' associations did not wait for a clarification of the conflicting reports on the incident. Instead, they launched a nation-wide campaign, including full page advertisements in newspapers, against the "Communist subversion" organized by priests in general and Jesuits in particular. While Archbishop Chávez y González defended the priests, the government sent troops into Aguilares and the surrounding countryside. The results were harsh:

> Two ex-Jesuit seminarians working with the Aguilares peasants were expelled, as was a Colombian parish priest; a former Jesuit, Juan José Ramírez, was interrogated, beaten and tortured with electric shocks for ten days. The government also expelled two foreign missionaries working in the San Salvador slums, Belgian Willbrord Denaux and U.S. Maryknoll missioner Bernard Survil. Before being deported, Denaux was shackled to the metal springs of a bed during twenty hours of interrogation.[5]

The attacks on the Church weren't over. On March 12, 1977, during the state of siege and repression that followed demonstrations against the fraudulent presidential election that year, Father Rutilio Grande was shot to death. He had been on his way to say Mass at El Paisnal, and died together with a teenage helper and a seventy-two-year old peasant.

By 1977 the violence that escalated against the Church for its support of peasant organization and agrarian reform formed part of a nation-wide, government-sponsored repression of unions, teachers' associations, dissident politicians, indeed all of the institutions of civil society. It was in 1977 that Molina's Minister of Defence, General Carlos Humberto Romero, became President in "elections" which were scandalously fraudulent and held in the midst of widespread repression.[6] General Romero represented the most retrograde members of the oligarchy — who now appeared to have gained the political initiative and were prepared to physically eliminate opposition and all forms of independent popular organization, even the politically moderate.

Another activist priest who had been spreading the gospel of equality, Father Alfonso Navarro, was killed May 11, 1977 by the White Warriors Union (UGB),* one of the smaller right-wing vigilante organizations. The act was carried out in reprisal for the kidnapping and murder of Foreign Minister Mauricio Borgonovo, a member of one of the "Fourteen Families". Borgonovo had been killed by the Popular Forces of

* Unión Guerrera Blanca.

Liberation — Farabundo Martí (FPL-FM),* one of the three guerrilla organizations functioning by that time. The UGB then went on to threaten all Jesuits working in El Salvador with death if they did not leave the country by July 21. The priests, the UGB announced, would be considered "military targets" and systematically eliminated.[7] Anonymous pamphlets circulated, urging people to "Be a patriot! Kill a priest!" The vigilante organization was believed to be linked to one of the landowners' associations, the Eastern Region Farmer's Front (FARO)† which had been instrumental in blocking the implementation of a very mild Agrarian Reform enacted in 1976 by Colonel Molina's government.[8] At this time as well, in a sequence of events that were to repeat themselves with terrifying regularity, San Salvador auxiliary Bishop Arturo Rivera y Damas, his life threatened, was forced into hiding. Other priests had to leave their parishes to take refuge in the archbishop's offices, or flee the country. The Jesuit University in San Salvador was bombed six times and the UGB "warned parents that any student attending the city's five Jesuit schools might be killed. All this because the Jesuits had supported Molina's half-hearted attempts at agrarian reform."[9]

The Church's militancy and commitment under repression were remarkable. Upon stepping down from the Archbishop's Office, seventy-six-year old Chávez y González asked to be appointed parish priest of Suchitoto because the town's two priests had been forced to "flee the country after receiving death threats from the White Warriors".[10]

A priest explained what the peasants in the Aguilares area learned from these events:

> The administrators of haciendas refused jobs to people who were organized; informers denounced them to foremen and officials; the authorities did not recognize their unions. The crude reality taught them that the defence of their human rights was going to be a long, hard struggle. Those who cause this struggle have vested interests and they are unmoved by the plight of the peasant.[11]

But it was not only the peasants who learned this. Many conservative clerics were radicalized as they worked in urban shantytowns as well as in the peasant villages, and a few later even joined the guerrilla organizations. A Spanish priest described his political transformation to Tom Buckley:

> I am by birth and training a conservative, but in my twelve years in El Salvador I have been radicalized — not that I like that term. To me, the dividing line is whether or not you have human sensibility. I will tell you how anti-Communist I used to be: I regretted that the Bay of Pigs invasion did not succeed; I was happy when your

---

* Fuerzas Populares de Liberación — Farabundo Martí.
† Frente de Agricultoros de la Región Oriental.

Marines landed in the Dominican Republic; it didn't even bother
me when Allende committed "suicide", as your government said. I
admit I was wrong. And I will tell you something else. I wish the
gringos to be beaten here. . . .
   I said to your Ambassador [Robert] White last November [1980],
after the leaders of the Democratic Revolutionary Front had been
taken from our San José high school and murdered: "This is Vietnam." It is! It is true that I favor the poor against the oligarchs. I am
against violence, but even more against unjust violence. There is
another matanza going on in the countryside. If the solution to this
is Marxism, let it come, rather than what is here.[12]

The Guerrilla Armies and New Forms of Popular Organization

By the end of 1975, three guerrilla organizations were established, all
linked to the new forms of popular organization that were emerging
with the repression.[13] The oldest, the Popular Forces of Liberation —
Farabundo Martí (FPL-FM), had been founded in 1970. It emerged in a
split from the Communist Party of El Salvador (PCS), which had never
achieved legal status because of its role in the Peasant Rebellion of
1932, and which had been pursuing a policy of alliances with moderate
reformist political parties such as the Christian Democrats and the social
democratic MNR. The FPL-FM, under the leadership of long-time PCS Secretary General Cayetano Carpio, drew its leadership from radicalized
sectors of the labour movement and from the universities.
   The second guerrilla organization, the Popular Revolutionary Army
(ERP),* was founded in 1971 by radical Christians, primarily university
students associated with the Christian Democratic Party. The third, the
Armed Forces of National Resistance (FARN),† emerged as a split from
the ERP in 1975. A fourth guerrilla organization, the Revolutionary Party
of Central American Workers (PRTC),** was founded after General
Romero's overthrow in 1979.
   The FPL-FM directed its activities "against the economic elite and
ORDEN", the ERP "against members of the government security forces"
and the FARN "raised considerable funds and gained the most international notoriety through abductions of members of the international
business community".[14] Until the late 1970s guerrillas had the capacity
to carry out only "small scattered actions against the security forces,
retaliations against government spies and torturers, and kidnappings for
ransom".[15] But with the ever-escalating repression, particularly after the
ascension of General Carlos Romero to power, their organizational ties
with the population were cemented.

* Ejército Revolucionario del Pueblo.
† Fuerzas Armadas de Resistencia Nacional.
** Partido Revolucionario de Los Trabajadores Centroamericanos.

Specifically, the guerrilla organizations' capacities and influence developed in conjunction with linkages they established with a number of broadly-based and loosely-structured political coalitions. These coalitions replaced the political party organizations that had developed in the 1960s and that were essentially destroyed in the escalating repression following the 1972 Presidential "elections". The coalitions were built on a large number of small grass-roots associations representing particular sectors of society: peasants, industrial workers, shantytown dwellers, teachers, university students and so on. The guerrilla organizations, of course, also aided in the constitution of these associations and the subsequent coalitions, working at the grass-roots level much as the radical clergy did, building "wells and roads to inaccessible villages", forming cooperatives and teaching peasants to read.[16]

The largest of the coalitions, the Popular Revolutionary Bloc (BPR),* was founded in 1975 and associated itself with the oldest of the guerrilla organizations, the FPL-FM. The BPR or *Bloque,* brought together the Christian Federation of Salvadorean Peasants (FECCAS), the Federation of Rural Workers (FTC),† the National Teachers Association (ANDES),** the Union of Slum Dwellers, the Union Coordinating Committee made up of more than fifty industrial unions, the Association of University Professors and three federations of university and secondary school students.[17] The programme and political orientation of the *Bloque* was socialist. To publicize its goals and recruit members in the absence of legal guarantees and honest elections, the *Bloque* engaged in "a campaign of nonviolent, dramatic activities of civil disobedience", including street theatre.[18]

The three other smaller coalitions were similarly structured. The United Popular Action Front (FAPU),†† founded in 1974 and later associated with the FARN, also brought together associations of peasants, urban workers, teachers and students. The Popular Leagues — 28th of February (LP-28),*** a student-dominated coalition established in 1977, supported the ERP. That coalition took its name from the date in 1977 on which the security forces killed more than one hundred demonstrators protesting the fraudulent "election" of General Romero to the presidency.[19] Finally, the Popular Liberation Movement (MLP)††† was organized jointly with the PRTC in 1979.

After the failure of the October 15 junta which overthrew General Romero in 1979 (see below), the Communist Party of El Salvador also opted for a military revolutionary strategy. It joined with these organiza-

---

* *Bloque Popular Revolucionario.*
† *Federación de Trabajadores Campestres.*
** *Asociación Nacional de Educadores Salvadoreños.*
†† *Frente de Acción Popular Unificada.*
*** *Ligas Populares 28 de Febrero.*
††† *Movimiento de Liberación Popular.*

tions in January 1980 to form the Unified Revolutionary Directorate, an important step in the ultimate creation of the Democratic Revolutionary Front/Farabundo Martí National Liberation Front (FDR/FMLN) coalition that brought together the revolutionary opposition into one body (see Table VIII).

Table VIII
The Popular and Associated Guerrilla Organizations

Guerrilla Organizations	Popular Organizations
1. Popular Forces of Liberation — Farabundo Martí (FPL-FM); founded 1970	1. Popular Revolutionary Bloc (BPR); founded 1975
2. Popular Revolutionary Army (ERP); founded 1971	2. Popular Leagues — 28th of February (LP-28); founded 1977
3. Armed Forces of National Resistance (FARN); founded 1975	3. United Popular Action Front (FAPU); founded 1974
4. Revolutionary Party of Central American Workers (PRTC); founded 1979	4. Popular Liberation Movement (MLP); founded 1979
Organizations 1-3, in combination with the Communist Party of El Salvador (PCS), formed the Unified Revolutionary Directorate (DRU) in January 1980 to coordinate action. The PRTC joined later. In October 1980, the command structures were unified and the *Farabundo Martí National Liberation Front* (FMLN) was established.	Organizations 1-3, in combination with Democratic Nationalist Union (UDN), signed a declaration of unity establishing the Movement for Popular Unity (MUP) on January 11, 1980. The Revolutionary Coordination of the Masses (the *Coordinadora*) was established, composed of the top leadership of the various organizations. Somewhat later, the MLP also entered the *Coordinadora*. The MUP was joined by the social democratic MNR and the Popular Social Christian Movement (MPSC), (a split from the PDC), and a number of associations and unions to form the Democratic Revolutionary Front (FDR) on April 18, 1980.

Sources: Arnson, *Background Information on the Security Forces in El Salvador and U.S. Military Assistance, I.P.S.,* Sol, *Para Entender El Salvador,* and *Central America Update.*

For its part, the government had tried unsuccessfully to halt the success of revolutionary movements in the rural areas by integrating its own creation, the Salvadorean Communal Union (UCS)* of peasants,

* *Unión Comunal Salvadoreña.*

with ORDEN.[20] The regime, in short, had only repressive solutions to the crisis.

While the guerrilla organizations and their associated popular coalitions represented various currents of Marxist and radical Christian thought, Archbishop Oscar Arnulfo Romero y Galdames and his predecessor Chávez y González lent a moral unity to the opposition. Oscar Romero, no relation to the General whose regime he fought from the pulpit, was elevated to the Archbishop's office soon after the electoral farce of 1977. Not only did he consistently and strongly defend the people's right to organize, but he also documented and condemned the repression through the Archbishop's Legal Aid Office. In 1978, he declared the right of insurrection:

> When a dictatorship seriously violates human rights and attacks the common good of the nation, when it becomes unbearable and closes all channels of dialogue, of understanding, of rationality — when this happens, the church speaks of the legitimate right of insurrectional violence.[21]

Finally, a day before his assassination on March 24, 1980, he urged the armed forces and the police to lay down their arms.

The October Coup and the Disintegration of the Reformist Junta

While the repression of the Molina years (1972-1977) was tolerable to the United States, the extensive and indiscriminate violence unleashed by General Romero ultimately became an embarrassment to the Administration of Jimmy Carter. The United States had not reacted to the electoral frauds perpetrated in 1972 and in 1977, although the Christian Democratic Party had protested in Washington as well as in El Salvador. American military assistance and its economic aid programme remained unaffected. Foreign capital continued to flow in as the old initiatives to industrial investment were improved and a new free-trade zone, San Bartolo, was established.[22]

Nevertheless, the political crisis deepened in a deteriorating economic situation. In spite of new foreign investment, the underlying structural crisis of the economy did not lessen, but instead worsened with the rapid price rises of petroleum imports and the fall in the price of coffee during the second half of the decade. A study by the United Nations Economic Commission for Latin America (ECLA) laconically noted that in 1977 the "real income of salaried workers declined".[23]

Finally, as El Salvador established a dubious track record of condemnations by international human rights organizations,* and even the

---

*See International Commission of Jurists, Review, "El Salvador" (June 1978); Organization of American States, Inter-American Commission on Human Rights, Report on the Situation of Human Rights in El Salvador, (Washington, D.C., 1979); and Amnesty International.

Carter administration began to criticize the astounding scale and brutality of the repression, General Romero took the initiative. During his first year in office, the General "joined [the repressive military regimes in] Argentina, Brazil and Guatemala in rejecting proposed U.S. military assistance, in protest over American criticism of its human rights record".[24]

It took the fear of spreading revolution, brought home by the Sandinista's victory in Nicaragua in July of 1979, to move the United States into action. It was thus with the blessing of the Carter administration that an apparently reformist military-civilian junta entered the executive office in San Salvador through a coup d'état on October 15, 1979. As it turned out, the civilian members of the junta were never actually permitted to exercise power. The opportunity for initiating a step-by-step peaceful transformation of the system, it seemed, had been lost in 1972.

A small progressive faction of younger officers momentarily gained the initiative on October 15, sending Romero and fifty hard-line officers into exile. These younger officers organized a civilian-military junta composed of Ramón Mayorga (rector of the Catholic University), Guillermo Ungo (Secretary General of the social-democratic MNR), Mario Andino (representative of the private sector), Colonel Adolfo Majano (a widely respected and politically independent officer) and Colonel Jaime Gutierrez (a conservative pro-American officer). The cabinet included a wide spectrum of representatives from the country's progressive opposition parties. However, Colonel Guillermo García, a hard-line opponent of the popular organizations that had emerged in the 1970s, was appointed Minister of Defence and Public Security. Ungo represented the Popular Forum in the junta. The Popular Forum "had been formed to oppose the Romero government [and] included both the Christian and Social Democrats [the MNR], unions, professional associations, and the mass organizations".[25]

By late 1981, only Colonels Gutierrez and García, and none of the popular organizations, were to remain in the thrice reconstituted junta, by that time headed by José Napoleón Duarte. By January 3, 1980, all the civilians had resigned to protest the escalation of violence by security forces and paramilitary organizations supported by the oligarchy and integrated with sectors of the regular armed forces. The progressive officers could not maintain their ascendancy. The day following the coup:

> *A large and heavily armed contingent of combined security forces, accompanied by armored vehicles, broke into the locales of four groups of striking workers in the capital, killing seven, wounding and beating an undetermined number, and detaining 90. On October 16 and 17, in four rural towns peaceful mass meetings were attacked by security forces leaving 50 dead, 60 wounded and a large number of persons detained. On October 21 and 22 in San Salvador, assaults on two mass meetings left three dead and several*

wounded. A peaceful demonstration on October 29, called to pro-
test earlier violence, was attacked by security forces and resulted in
65 persons killed, hundreds wounded and a large number detained.
Two days later, a group giving a comic street play mocking the
Government was trapped and fired upon in the central market area
by heavily armed Treasury Police, who killed 30 players and
onlookers, and wounded dozens.[26]

In the following months, these repressive actions repeated themselves
with deadening regularity. They were documented by the Archdiocesan
Office of Legal Assistance, which repeatedly pointed to the culpability
of the security forces rather than — as the Minister of Defence claimed
— of guerrilla instigators. According to information compiled by
Church and human rights organizations, the security forces alone "were
responsible for more than 200 deaths" in two months, dashing the
hopes raised by the October coup. ORDEN, despite its formal dissolution,
continued to kidnap, torture, mutilate and kill.[27]

The internationally-respected civilians in the October junta found
that they were being used as a reformist camouflage to keep repression
out of sight of the rest of the world. Unable to control the armed forces
or to persuade the landlord class to accept necessary reforms — specifically, a genuine agrarian reform and a sharing of political power with
the country's popular organizations — they resigned. By the end of
January, the five progressive officers who had instigated the October 15
coup had also been driven into exile. The descent into full-scale civil
war could no longer be halted.

A new junta was organized on January 9, 1980. Christian Democrats
José Antonio Morales Ehrlich (former mayor of San Salvador) and Hector Dada Hirezi stepped in to replace the civilians who had resigned.*
By March 3, Dada Hirezi had realized that effective power remained in
the hands of military and paramilitary organizations backed by the
oligarchy. In a letter of resignation he declared:

The Junta is incapable of taking action against those whom I see as
the principal opponents of the process, and it is clearer every day
that they are firmly ensconced in the very structures of the govern-
ment. . . .

I shall not go into further detail about my interpretations: the facts
themselves are the indisputable proof of the conclusion. We have
been unable to stop the repression, and those who commit acts of
repression, in defiance of the junta's authority, remain unpunished;
the promised dialogue with the popular organizations has not come
about; the possibilities of generating reforms supported by the peo-
ple have retreated beyond our grasp.[28]

---

* This reconstructed junta will be referred to here as the Military-Christian
Democratic junta.

On March 5, José Napoleón Duarte agreed to replace Dada Hirezi in the junta, as all the while resignations from cabinet positions continued (see Appendix I).

The Unification of the Revolutionary Opposition

The progressive political organizations that had been represented in the October junta, and the revolutionary popular organizations that had captured the mass base of the electoral parties during the course of the post-1972 repression, began the difficult process of unification in January 1980 (see Table VIII). On the 11th, a new coalition, called the Movement for National Unity (MUP) came together. It included the Popular Revolutionary Bloc (BPR), the United Popular Action Front (FAPU) and the Popular Leagues — 28th of February (LP-28), as well as the Communist Party-associated Democratic Nationalist Union (UDN), which had formed part of the October junta. The top leadership of these organizations constituted themselves into the Revolutionary Coordination of the Masses, the *Coordinadora* for short. Simultaneously, in combination with the Communist Party of El Salvador, the guerrilla organizations formed the Unified Revolutionary Directorate (DRU) to coordinate military action.

The decision to join the armed struggle represented a radically new departure for the CPS. Like other Latin American Communist parties, it had lent its support in the 1970s to the attempts to create electoral fronts and influence progressive sectors of the military. In late 1980, the CPS joined other Central American Communist Parties in recognizing that they "were not necessarily the vanguard of social change, but rather one revolutionary force among many. . . . The parties emphasized the need for unity among the revolutionary forces [in which the Communists are numerically in a minority], and the place of armed struggle among other forms of political activity."[29]*

In the following months, the *Coordinadora* was joined by other political organizations represented in the October junta. In early April, Social Democrats, dissident Christian Democrats, civic associations, professional and labour groups joined together in the Democratic Front.† The Popular Faction of the Christian Democratic Party had

* The CIA's *National Basic Intelligence Factbook,* January 1980, estimated that the CPS had 220 to 225 active members and 5,000 sympathizers.[30]
† The Democratic Front was made up of the National Revolutionary Movement (MNR-social democratic), the Popular Social Christian Movement (MPSC), the National University of El Salvador (UES), the Association of University Students (AGEUS), the Independent Movement of Professionals and Technicians (MIPIES), the Association of Bus Companies of El Salvador (AEAS), the Federation of Salvadorean Workers (FENASTRAS), the Federation of Food, Clothing and Textile Workers (FESTIAVISCES), the Revolutionary Federation of Unions (FSR), the United

organized itself into the Popular Social Christian Movement after withdrawing from the PDC's national convention on March 10. The faction
"held 20 per cent of the convention's delegates".[32] Then, on April 18,
the Democratic Front joined with the *Coordinadora,* adopting its programme (see Appendix III) and forming the Democratic Revolutionary
Front (FDR), which now leads the political opposition in El Salvador. The
FDR's military arm, the successor to the Directorate (DRU), is the
Farabundo Martí National Liberation Front (FMLN), named after the best
known of the Communist leaders involved in the 1932 Peasant Rebellion. The FMLN was to provide tighter coordination and a unified command structure for the guerrilla organizations.

On June 13, 1980, the social democratic parties of the world
endorsed the FDR at a meeting in Oslo, Norway. The Oslo declaration
stated:

> The Socialist International fully supports the struggle of the Frente
> Democrático Revolucionario for freedom and democracy in El Sal-
> vador. . . . The Socialist International asks the United States' gov-
> ernment to consider that support for the junta in El Salvador is not a
> viable solution and will not prevent further bloodshed. We call on
> the U.S. to change its policies. This is not anti-Americanism but an
> effort to achieve a constructive relationship between the U.S. and
> the countries of Central America.

It was under the auspices of the Socialist International that Canadian
New Democratic Party leader Ed Broadbent undertook his unfortunately
unsuccessful mediation mission in May and June 1981. Neither the
Duarte nor the U.S. governments were willing to sit down at the bargaining table.[33]

The broad social and political base of the FDR makes it akin to
Europe's World War II movements against fascism. According to a
former American Ambassador to El Salvador (January 1961 to July
1964), Murat W. Williams, this "heterogeneous left must make up
eighty per cent of the Salvadorean population".[34] It is precisely because
of this broad base and its political pluralism or "heterogeneity" that the
FDR enjoys the support of the world's social democratic parties and
broad sectors of the Christian Churches.

In fact, the revolutionary coalition became broader and broader as
the failure of the October 15 junta, and the continuing atrocities perpetrated by the state's security forces, convinced social democrats and
progressive Christian Democrats that no reform programme could suc-
ceed without first dismantling the paramilitary organizations and the
National Guard, and completely reorganizing the army. In order to
achieve this, the revolutionary opposition had to build a military power
of its own, based on the guerrilla armies of the FMLN.

Federation of Unions of El Salvador (FUSS), the Union of Social Security Workers
(STISS), and the Union of Workers of United Industries (SIIUSA).[31]

The Repressive "Reforms" of the Military-Christian Democratic Junta

While the revolutionary opposition forces united in the FDR/FMLN during 1980, the Military-Christian Democratic junta's internal power base narrowed. The Reagan administration effectively worked to keep it in power by insisting on a Christian Democratic civilian presence in the junta (there are members of the military who would prefer to govern alone) and by providing increasing quantities of military and economic aid. With more and better weapons, the level of violence also escalated: more than 2,000 people were now dying every month in this new *matanza*.

The new level of violence did not simply stem from more frequent military engagements with the guerrilla armies, although that is one source. It stemmed, to a large extent, from the junta's agrarian reform programme, announced on March 6, 1980. Reform was to be carried out in three phases. The first consisted of the expropriation and formation into cooperatives of eighty per cent of the lands in estates over 500 hectares large. These lands made up approximately fifteen per cent of El Salvador's arable soil. The second phase was intended to break up the 150- to 500-hectare estates of the coffee oligarchy. This would affect more than sixty per cent of coffee production. The third phase involved the conversion of tenants of small plots into owners of that same property. In fact those tenants often rented their plots from small property holders. Even if carried out to the letter of the law, the real distributive impact of the agrarian reform was questionable (see Appendix IV). But the way in which its implementation was started contradicted its goal entirely.

The second and most significant phase was soon indefinitely postponed. Worse yet, simultaneously with the enactment of agrarian reform, a state of siege was declared, which effectively placed the armed forces in charge of implementation. Military units were immediately dispatched to occupy *haciendas*, a move hailed by U.S. government sources as an indication of the junta's seriousness. While some *haciendas* were in fact cooperativized, the military also proceeded to terrorize peasant organizations and physically eliminate their leaderships.

The Legal Aid Office of the Archdiocese of San Salvador reported that the military invaded peasant zones and settlements 380 times between January 1 and July 13, 1980, burning and destroying peasant houses on all but sixty-six of these occasions. On June 15, eight provincial executive councils of the Salvadorean Communal Union (UCS),* a politically moderate peasant organization founded by the AFL-CIO-sponsored American Institute for Free Labor Development (AIFLD),

* *Unión Salvadoreña Comunal.*

protested the violence associated with the land reform. During 1980, more than 200 cooperative leaders were reported killed. Officials of the Institute of Agrarian Reform (ISTA) have described how army units, accompanied by members of ORDEN, organized elections in a cooperative and then proceeded to execute the elected leaders.

Army officers and members of right-wing paramilitary groups have also organized protection rackets and other corrupt practices in the areas where estates have come under land reform.[35] Thus, *The New York Times* reports that "the military also has done some confiscating of its own. One large farm not included in the Government expropriation plan was taken over by officers and soldiers from the local command. They occupied the former owner's house, removed much of the furniture to military headquarters and sold crops for their own benefit. The family was eventually able to recover the land but is now obliged to pay the soldiers several hundred dollars a month to leave the property alone."[36] In short, more of the peasant-produced surplus now goes to the military, which consequently has become even more of a caste. Peasants on most estates that have been "cooperativized" have benefited only marginally or not at all. The January 3, 1981 assassination of the head of ISTA, José Rodolfo Viera, along with two American AIFLD consultants, was yet another incident in the long chain of violence sparked by the agrarian reform. Viera had attempted to expose the corrupt practices of the military agrarian "reformers".[37]

The spate of resignations from the Duarte-led Military-Christian Democratic junta in the spring of 1980 was to a great extent provoked by cabinet members realizing that the security forces and paramilitary organizations had found in the agrarian reform yet another means for enhancing their own power. Explaining his resignation of March 26, the Under-Secretary of Agriculture, Jorge Villacorta, stated that the majority of the dead in the civil war were "peasants or militants of popular organizations, whom the security forces and sectors of the army consider their principal enemies". Villacorta went on:

> I resigned from my position ... because I believe it is useless to continue in a government not only incapable of putting an end to violence but a government which itself is generating the political violence through repression. . . . In reality from the first moment that the implementation of the agrarian reform began, what we saw was a sharp increase in official violence against the very peasants who were the supposed "beneficiaries" of the process. . . .
>
> During the first days of the reform — to cite one case — five directors and two presidents of new campesino organizations were assassinated and I am informed that the repressive practice continues to increase. Recently, on one of the haciendas of the agrarian reform, uniformed members of the security forces accompanied by someone with a mask over his face, brought the workers together; the masked man was giving orders to the person in charge of the

troops and these campesinos *were gunned down in front of their co-workers. These bloody acts have been carried out by uniformed members of the National Guard and the Hacienda Police, accompanied by civilian members of* ORDEN, *all heavily armed, including support from tanks and heavy equipment. With these crimes, the effects of the agrarian reform are lost.* [38]

Even if the agrarian reform decree could be fully applied in a climate of peace and order — wishful thinking in the present power structure — its benefits would be severely limited. The poorest majority of the rural population would be excluded from any benefits, since the law applies only to those who have some access to land and permanent employment on estates, or both (see Table IV). Much coffee land would remain unaffected, and therefore El Salvador's oligarchy would retain a substantial measure of its socio-economic and political power. It must be stressed that, because there are no economies of scale involved, coffee production is not necessarily more efficiently carried out on large estates; in fact, coffee is efficiently and productively cultivated on small family farms in many parts of the world.

The inadequacy of the agrarian reform, even in the best of circumstances, for responding to the conditions of misery and unemployment in the countryside has been carefully documented by the independent aid agency OXFAM (See Appendix IV). Two weeks before his assassination, Archbishop Romero warned:

If it is not possible that these measures exclude every form of repression of the peasants, if it is not possible that these reforms be carried out by the people — the organized as well as the unorganized — these reforms will not have resolved the problem, and their failure will be converted into a new weapon by which the oligarchy will triumphantly return, saying that they alone are capable of saving the nation. [39]

While the escalation of violence in the rural areas following the declaration of the state of siege on March 5, 1980, was dramatic, the cities were not spared either. Between January 1, and July 13, 1980, the Legal Aid Office of the Archdiocese identified seventy-seven army raids and sackings of union and student locales, democratic institutions, offices of the Church and the Archdiocese. The Legal Aid Office also documented 128 machine-gunning and dynamite attacks against the same type of offices during this period. Following a pattern similar to the countryside, places of work in the cities were militarized in August 1980, following widespread protests and strikes. The murders of opposition leaders also continued. In November 1980, government security forces assassinated the FDR's first president, social democrat Enrique Alvarez, former Minister of Agriculture in the October junta, along with other prominent members of the Front.

Table IX
The Targets of Repression and Those Responsible, 1980

Assassinations Jan. 1 - Dec. 31, 1980   May 1980 - Jan. 1981: Those Responsible

Campesinos	3272	National Guard	534
Workers	392	National Police	169
Students	724	Treasury Police	31
Teachers	136	Civilian Dressed	184
Paramedics	5	Combined Armed Forces	2930
Mayors	2	Army	131
Professionals	42	ORDEN	109
Slum Dwellers	24	Death Squad	752
Employees	352	Secret Anti-Communist Army	4
Religious (male)	5	Special Anti-Communist Brigades	2
Religious (female)	5	Not identified	1752
Transp. workers	7		
Businessmen	170		
Not identified	2340		

From the report 58% were known to have been carried out by the military forces, 16% by the paramilitary forces and 26% could not be identified, although they followed a similar pattern of killings.

Note: This does not include the 3,400 campesinos massacred in major operations by the Salvadorean Army at Sumpul, Trifinio, San Vicente and Morazán.

— from Report of the Socorro Juridico, Legal Office of the Archdiocese of San Salvador

Source: Latin American and Caribbean Labour Report, (Toronto: LAWG, March 1981).

The violence of the governing junta became, then, constant, omnipresent and brutal (see Table IX). It was to be directed against all forms of popular organization — the neighbourhood councils first set up under Duarte's aegis as mayor in the slums and shantytowns of San Salvador, religious groups, urban unions and peasant associations of all political stripes, anyone who dared to question what was taking place. The violence was the reason why the areas of guerrilla influence and territorial control continued to grow. What alternative is there to the military defeat of the security forces and paramilitary organizations that support the rule of the few who began to reorganize El Salvador's economy and society for their own benefit beginning in the 1880s?

In addition to more military repression, the alternative proposed by Duarte and the U.S. government was "free elections" in 1982 and 1983. But who would participate? Within the power structure as constituted, it would be suicidal for the representatives of the popular organizations to present themselves in an election campaign. This has been recognized by the country's legal association, which has refused to participate in the formulation of an electoral law.[40] Duarte himself admitted that "As things stand now, it was unlikely that the left or even some elements of the Christian Democrats would participate."[41] That left, as Murat Williams pointed out, is heterogeneous and makes up 80 per cent of the population — those excluded by the historical pattern of El Salvador's economic development as well as responsible members of the middle class who have said no to continuation of rule by and for the military-oligarchic coalitions that have dominated the country since 1931.

The willingness of Duarte and other Christian Democrats to participate in the junta is somewhat of a puzzle. In trying to unravel it, writer Tom Buckley questioned both Duarte and his opponents. Buckley found that Duarte's opponents did not question the President's integrity. "But they say that his long exile put him hopelessly out of touch with developments in El Salvador — notably his party's loss of support — and that vanity, disappointment, and the belated emergence of, in Ungo's words, 'a personal obsession for power and his primitive anti-Communism' warped his judgement to the point where he was willing to enter the junta and then become its president."[42] According to Buckley, Duarte's opponents now see him as "little better than a puppet, trading on what remains of his reputation for the ultimate benefit of the armed forces and the oligarchy".

Of course, Duarte does not share his opponents' point of view. He believes that carrying out "intelligent" political change is something that "can't be done overnight". He told Buckley: "The army, as an institution, is willing to accept a political solution, but the others — the National Guard and the police — have been trained for fifty years to do it the other way, and it will take time to change them."[43] According to Duarte, the only way the military might immediately change would be if he threatened resignation. But recognizing that such a threat could backfire, Duarte added, "I won't bet everything I have on one card and take the chance of losing — but not just for myself. If I did, and lost, there would be half a million dead here."[44]

Leonel Gómez, a former ISTA official during Duarte's membership in the junta, challenges this interpretation of the army's flexibility: "There is an integrated officer corps. If its leadership truly wanted to eliminate substantially the abuses now occurring it could. But remember it doesn't. The army is bent on a war to exterminate all possible challenges to its power."[45] There is also the question of why, if Duarte is right, the army did not push for the political solution in 1972 when the circumstances were more propitious, and why the progressive officers who brought about the October 15 coup are now in exile.

The United States: Strategic Interests

José Napoleón Duarte, in fact, became a member of the junta in power because the United States insisted on it — to provide, as Archbishop

Romero argued, a façade of legitimacy.[46] The United States also insisted on the agrarian reform programme, which was largely authored by Dr. Roy Prosterman, a law professor at the University of Washington in Seattle. It was Prosterman who prepared the 1968 Vietnam Pacification Program, a combination of land reform with repression designed to undercut the Viet Cong's bases of popular support in the rural areas.[47] These policies, together with increasing military aid, were set into place under the Carter administration. During his last weeks in office, the outgoing President restored a $5 million military aid package which had been suspended following the murder of four American church women in December 1980. Carter also "authorized the placement of up to twenty American military trainers in El Salvador [not including the staff of the U.S. Military Group stationed at the Embassy in El Salvador]".[48]

Military aid commitments rose rapidly under the new Republican administration. By late March 1981, Reagan had approved $25 million in military credits and authorized the placement of fifty-six non-combat military advisers. The U.S. government was also considering troop commitments. Off-the-record interviews in Panama City led Globe and Mail correspondent Oakland Ross to conclude, "Unless there is a major improvement in the sagging fortunes of Government troops battling insurgents in El Salvador, the United States will soon be left with little choice but to send in its own fighting force."[49] The civil war as Ross saw it was a stalemate, with little likelihood that the Salvadorean security forces would soon be able to break out of the military impasse. U.S. military sources considered the situation to be "discouraging" and "lousy". According to Ross: "If it continues long enough, the stalemate will destroy the country's economy and lead to an eventual victory for the guerrillas, who are considered to have superior morale and better organization."[50] By all indications the United States has appeared determined to prevent that revolutionary victory at any cost.

At the same time, American military aid has been channelled to armed forces that have run amuck and rule through terror. Officers have turned over weapons to the paramilitary organizations such as ORDEN and to individuals such as Roberto D'Abuisson, a former intelligence officer widely believed to have organized the assassination of Archbishop Romero. D'Abuisson is so extreme in his right-wing views that he has accused Duarte of Communist sympathies and participated in a military conspiracy to overthrow him on March 4, 1981. He has since avoided the arrest that the government ordered. Confronted with the indiscriminate terrorism of the Salvadorean armed forces and the incapacity of the civilians in the junta to control them, Jeane J. Kirkpatrick, the Chief of the U.S. delegation to the United Nations, simply argued that this was "an absolutely normal condition for a Latin American government. Latin governments have traditionally been characterized by weak political institutions".[51] Former U.S. Ambassador to El

Salvador during the Carter administration, Robert E. White, speaking to Kirkpatrick, by contrast, argued against the "normalcy" of the situation and protested increasing military commitment:

> To the extent that you emphasize a military solution in El Salvador, you are going to be buttressing one of the most out-of-control, violent, bloodthirsty groups of men in the world. They have killed — at a minimum — 5,000 or 6,000 kids on the mere suspicion that they were involved with the leftists.[52]

Yet that is the solution for which the United States has effectively opted, while all the time the threat of the regionalization of the war increased. The realistic and progressive political alternative, negotiations with the FDR/FMLN that could lead to the dismantling of ORDEN and the National Guard, and an integration of the popular armies of the guerrillas with the remaining sane sectors of the regular army, have been rejected by the United States and, of course, Duarte. So, the second *matanza* continued unabated while the United States poured in the weapons to make it possible.

The economic stake of the United States in El Salvador is not great although American foreign investment has had a significant impact on the evolution of the country's urban economy, given its small size (see Chapter 4). Even Central America taken as a whole is of minor economic importance to the United States. "Less than 1 per cent of American exports are purchased by the region and U.S. direct foreign investment is calculated to be less than $1 billion in book value."[53] This is not to say that specific multinational corporations do not have profitable investments in the area. Such investments obviously exist and, together with local capital, the managers of those enterprises exert strong pressure on American foreign policy. However, the U.S. reaction to El Salvador's civil war has to be seen in a broader context.

The Carter and, much more so, Reagan administrations have perceived Central American revolutionary movements in terms of geopolitics and military strategy, as a part of a global conflict between a Communist East and a democratic capitalist West. The United States appears totally incapable of understanding or accepting the need for a radical form of decolonization in an area where it has been traditionally hegemonic. It has intervened consistently in the past to halt the development of nationalistic revolutionary movements. To mention cases from the post-World War II period only, it did so in Guatemala in 1954, providing the military aid that allowed internal reactionary groups to overthrow the democratically-elected government of Jacobo Arbenz. (In the course of land reform, the Arbenz government had expropriated non-utilized lands owned by the United Fruit Company.) It did so again in the Dominican Republic in 1965. U.S. intransigence gave the Cuban revolutionary nationalist movement no choice but to seek assistance from the Soviet Union. As René Dumont has argued, in 1959 in Cuba:

> *The United States passed upan unexpected historical opportunity to revise its policy toward the south of the continent. Recognizing the Cuban Revolution was in a sense tantamount to accepting a radical form of decolonization, analogous in certain respects to that being carried out by France in Africa during this same period, this meant chalking up to profit and loss a certain number of investments in Cuba, many of them too highly amortized. The French did not ask Mali to reimburse them for the money — a considerable amount, expended on the hydraulic, agricultural and industrial improvements made by the Niger Authority. [For the U.S.] to ask for reimbursement at 1958 prices of latifundia, part of which had been bought for a few dollars per hectare in the period 1900 to 1910 seems, at the very least, to be a curious form of "aid to underdeveloped countries".*[54]

It is apparent that the United States had continued to repeat the mistakes of the past, and not only in El Salvador. Since the Nicaraguan revolution, that country has gradually been cut off from its normal trade relationships with the United States, not to mention aid and credit for reconstructing its war-torn economy.[55]

The Alternative: A Revolution Led by the FDR/FMLN

The revolutionary coalition of the FDR/FMLN, as already noted, brought together a broad and heterogeneous spectrum of progressive political forces, ranging from social democrats and radical Christians to orthodox and not-at-all-orthodox Marxists. The Communist Party of El Salvador, the smallest of the five guerrilla organizations today, is clearly pro-Soviet in its ideological orientation, but the revolutionary movement as a whole represents indigenous forms of nationalism and socialism. As argued here, that movement developed in a decentralized fashion during the 1970s in response to concrete socio-economic and political conditions that prevailed in El Salvador. Its forms of organization were based on a multiplicity of popular associations and initiatives; its specific reform proposals arose from the experiences of those years and from an analysis of the prevailing system's incapacity to respond to the basic needs of the great majority of the population.

The programme and goals of the FDR/FMLN are akin to the policies being implemented by Nicaragua's revolutionary government.[56] Those include: a non-aligned foreign policy and the maintenance of a pluralistic political framework; the organization of a mixed economy structured on state ownership of basic sectors combined with private and cooperative enterprise in agriculture, retail commerce, and so on. The FDR/FMLN also intends to carry out a thorough-going agrarian reform to redistribute productive property and generate employment in the rural areas (see Appendix III). That agrarian reform could be considerably more radical than the one implemented in Nicaragua, because rural conditions in El Salvador have developed in particularly distorted ways.

The FDR/FMLN programme has been worked out in heated debates among the different revolutionary organizations that make up the coalition, and it has also been significantly influenced by contemporary radical Christian thought. This could happen precisely because of the Catholic clergy's grass-roots involvement in organizing unions and social action programmes both in the countryside and the cities. The Catholic Church of El Salvador, in fact, has played a pivotal role in the development of the revolution by defending popular organizations, demanding reforms, denouncing the repression of the regime, and asking the United States to halt its military aid programme.[57]

It has been these years of organizational work, combined with its ideological pluralism and indigeneous character, that permit the FDR/ FMLN to count on the active support of ever larger sectors of the Salvadorean population. *Maclean's* magazine, for example, interviewed PRTC leader Fabio Castillo and concluded that he is "a genuine, indigenous, Central American leftist" who is neither a "Soviet puppet nor an innocent victim" and that he is also "the very stuff of which American paranoia about Central America is made".[58]

In January of 1981, the FMLN conducted its first major military offensive against the Military-Christian Democratic junta. The offensive also constituted the first operational test of the unified command structure which had been established only three months before, in October 1980. Although widely reported as a failure in the U.S. press, the FMLN offensive, in fact, appears to have increased the territory under the control of the revolutionary forces and enhanced their military effectiveness through the experience provided in coordinating actions all over the country. Among the more spectacular of the offensive's victories was the desertion of "half the soldiers in the military barracks of Santa Ana, El Salvador's second largest city, . . . to the rebel army". The soldiers, of course, carried "their arms and ammunition with them".[59] In March, British journalist Jon Snow was inside guerrilla-controlled territory, which the army had supposedly cleared two weeks earlier:

> [Snow saw] *several hundred guerrillas undergoing training, and was told that there were about 1,000 in the immediate vicinity. The arms he saw had been captured from the army, and the military training was being given by Salvadoreans who had served in the regular army.*
>
> *Snow was able to contrast the relationship between the guerrillas and the local people with the reception the army had been given in the same area. He described the interdependence between them, and how the guerrillas' doctors tend the local population, in exchange for food. Many of the people in the area have suffered the brutality of the right-wing death squads and the national guard.*
>
> *By contrast, he said, the army can never afford to stay long in the areas they have temporarily cleared, because the local people sim-*

ply leave and will do nothing to assist their stay. The army has neither the manpower nor the popularity to hold these country areas.[60]

It is precisely the failures of, and lack of popular support for, the security forces during the January offensive that prompted an escalation of U.S. military aid. An American military official in Panama recently told a *Globe and Mail* correspondent that the junta "'might have gone down already had it not been for the renewal of U.S. military supplies during the failed offensive by guerrillas in January".[61]

Publicly, the United States justified its actions in the February "White Paper" on "Communist Interference in El Salvador" by asserting that "communist powers" were supplying massive quantities of arms to the revolutionary forces in an effort to take over the country. A reading of the documents appended to the "White Paper" actually indicates that the Soviet Union had refused to provide military assistance. Ethiopia and Vietnam had provided arms, and Cuba and Nicaragua had assisted in transporting them. Of these four Third World countries, only two have self-proclaimed Communist regimes. Moreover, the quantities of arms involved were not great. In fact, most of the weapons of the guerrillas were obtained from non-communist sources:

Even before November [1980] when weapons of Communist origin supposedly began to arrive in El Salvador in quantities, it was well known in international arms circles that the Salvadoreans were making extensive purchases in the international arms market. These purchases were made in part with the more than $50 million the guerrillas obtained from kidnappings [in the 1970s]. . . . Once these arms were acquired, they were sent in to El Salvador via Panama, Costa Rica, Honduras and Mexico as well as from Cuba and Nicaragua.[62]

The Salvadorean revolutionary forces, like insurgent movements elsewhere, capture arms and military equipment from their opposition. A variety of weapons (such as hand grenades, anti-tank grenades and contact mines) are locally produced, as indeed they were also by the Sandinistas in Nicaragua.[63] In West Germany and elsewhere in Europe, solidarity groups associated with social democratic parties have raised funds for the revolutionary opposition. The international sources of support for the FDR/FMLN, in sum, have been as heterogeneous and extensive as their internal bases of support.

Finally, it is relevant to ask whether the FDR/FMLN would have sought outside support if it were not for U.S. support and aid to the repressive regime in power in El Salvador.

As the civil war continued and extended itself territorially, the human costs reached more frightening proportions every day. In addition to the increasing numbers of casualties, the population as a whole has suffered the effects of the country's worst economic crisis since the

1930s. According to various estimates in 1980 the economy declined by 8 to 17 per cent, industry operated at 50 per cent below capacity, private fixed capital stood at 47.6 per cent of its 1978 level, the trade deficit reached $200 million, and the fighting in the rural areas created havoc for agriculture. In this situation, both unemployment and inflation have risen rapidly while small businesses, in particular, face bankruptcy.[64]

A victorious FDR/FMLN revolution would face great difficulties in reconstructing a war-torn economy and in reorganizing the country's socio-economic and political fabric to respond to popular needs. El Salvador is one of the poorest countries in Latin America and its present economic organization is among the most distorted. While the difficulties on the road to positive transformation would be great, the FDR/FMLN does address the country's basic problems of land reform, unemployment, dependency and exploitation by a rapacious minority. Writer Tom Buckley was recently "puzzled" by "the absolute refusal of the landowners, either out of cruelty, selfishness, indifference, or some sort of emotional or cultural blind spot, to pass on to their workers a reasonable share of their very large profits, even after events in Cuba and Nicaragua should have made it clear that the old order was passing for good".[65] It is clear that within the present regime of military-oligarchic dominance there is no possibility of material and cultural improvement for the great majority of the population.

And there is no foreseeable end to the civil war unless the United States stops its military aid and accepts negotiations. This is the alternative that Mexico, several European governments and most of the Salvadorean Church have proposed. They recognize the need for a radical transformation of the country's socio-economic and political structures, and the FDR/FMLN's potential for playing the leading role in achieving this.

Notes

[1] Leo Grande and Robbins (1980), p. 1087.
[2] Buckley (1981), p. 49.
[3] Lernoux (1980), p. 70.
[4] Cited in *Ibid.*
[5] *Ibid.,* p. 72.
[6] Webre (1979), p. 197.
[7] *Ibid.,* p. 200.
[8] Arnson (March 1980), p. 6.
[9] Lernoux (1980), p. 76.
[10] *Ibid.,* p. 77.
[11] Cited in *Ibid.,* p. 71.
[12] Buckley (1981), pp. 64, 66.
[13] The following discussion is drawn from a large number of primarily journalistic sources, including: the *Newsletter* of the Inter Church Committee on Human Rights in Latin America; *Central America Update;* Armstrong and Shenk (1980); Allman (1981); Arnson (March 1980); Buckley (1981); Wipfler (1980); and de Young (1981). It also relies on Menjíbar (1979 and 1980) and Gordon (1980).
[14] Arnson (March 1980), p. 11.
[15] Armstrong and Shenk (1980), p. 4.
[16] *Ibid.,* p. 4.
[17] Wipfler (1980), p. 118.
[18] *Ibid.*
[19] *Ibid.*
[20] Menjíbar (1979), p. 112.
[21] Cited in Buckley (1981), p. 64.
[22] Menjíbar (1979), pp. 108-109.
[23] Cited in *Ibid.,* p. 111.
[24] Arnson (March 1980), p. 8.
[25] Buckley (1981), p. 42.
[26] Wipfler (1980), p. 119.
[27] ICCHRLA (July-August 1980), p. 27.
[28] Cited in *Ibid.,* p. 37.
[29] *LAWR* (December 12, 1980).
[30] *Ibid.*
[31] Armstrong and Shenk (1980), p. 35.
[32] Arnson (June 1980), p. 4.
[33] See *The Globe and Mail* (June 6, 1981).
[34] *The New York Times* (December 29, 1980).
[35] Bonner (1981).
[36] *The New York Times* (August 16, 1981).
[37] Gómez in Subcommittee on Inter-American Affairs (1981), p. 195.
[38] Sections cited by Wheaton (1980), pp. 13-14; Arnson (June 1980), p. 4; and Simon and Stephens (1981), p. 29.
[39] Cited in Wipfler (1980), p. 121.
[40] *The Globe and Mail* (July 11, 1981).
[41] Buckley (1981), p. 50; see also *The New York Times* (August 16, 1981).
[42] Buckley (1981), p. 50.
[43] *Ibid.*

44 *Ibid.*
45 Subcommittee on Inter-American Affairs (1981), p. 197.
46 *The New York Times* (August 16, 1981).
47 Dowie (1981), p. 36.
48 Arnson (April 1981), p. 2; see also Appendix II.
49 *The Globe and Mail* (August 18, 1981).
50 *Ibid.*
51 Quoted in *Central America Update* (December 1980), p. 26.
52 *The New York Times* (March 8, 1981).
53 *Central America Update* (December 1980), p. 21.
54 Dumont (1970), p. 24; emphasis in the original.
55 *LAWR* (March 13 and 27, 1981, April 10, 1981); see *Central America Update* (December 1980) for a comprehensive analysis of U.S. policy in Central America.
56 For an analysis of events in Nicaragua, see Richard Fagen, *The Nicaraguan Revolution: A Personal Report* (Washington: Institute of Policy Studies, 1981).
57 ICCHRLA (July-August 1980).
58 *Maclean's* (June 15, 1981).
59 *Central America Update* (March 1981), p. 39; see also *The Globe and Mail,* (April 13, 1981).
60 *LAWR* (March 20, 1981).
61 *The Globe and Mail* (August 13, 1981).
62 *Central America Update* (March 1981), p. 39.
63 *Ibid.*; also, *The Globe and Mail* (February 28, 1981); *LAWR* (June 12, 1981).
64 *Central America Update* (June 1981), p. 48; see also *Maclean's* (June 15, 1981); and *The New York Times* (March 15, 1981).
65 Buckley (1981), p. 61.

Canadian Foreign Policy and El Salvador 7

by Tim Draimin

eginning in 1979, strong Canadian public reaction to the civil war in El Salvador has turned that conflict into a major issue for the federal government. This issue has affected Canada-United States relations, marred the first foray of President Ronald Reagan outside the United States and almost singlehandedly destroyed the public credibility of the Secretary of State for External Affairs, Mark Mac-Guigan.[1] Since Canadians' identification with their Latin American neighbours has historically been weak, this development has not only surprised Ottawa but has also brought into strong relief the passivity with which External Affairs often takes its lead from Washington when setting regional foreign policy.

The Canadian public began to be exposed to Latin American issues only in the 1970s, first with Salvador Allende's election (and subsequent overthrow) in Chile, later with the Sandinista insurrection in Nicaragua, most recently because of the struggle in El Salvador. Although most Canadians are completely dependent on U.S. news sources, with their sporadic and biased coverage of the hemisphere, strong bonds of solidarity link Canada with Latin America's anti-dictatorial and anti-imperialist struggles. Today Canadians are showing widespread public sympathy and support for the FDR/FMLN (Democratic Revolutionary Front/Farabundo Martí National Liberation Front) of El Salvador.

Financial Interest

For Canadian policy makers, El Salvador has simply been a part of Central America — a region which has rapidly developed significant commercial ties with Canada. Between 1970 and 1980, Canadian trade with the seven-nation isthmus grew by over 470 per cent reaching over $350 million annually.[2] The Central American region represents Canada's fifth most important trading partner in the hemisphere. The book value of Canadian investment there is placed at $300 million, although its real value could be almost five times that figure.[3] Canada's eagerness to exploit the expanding trade potential was evident in the Canadian International Development Agency's (CIDA) increasing involvement there over the past decade. While Central America represents only 6 per cent of Latin America's population, CIDA allocated fully 52 per cent of its regional budget to the region during 1978/79.

Traditional Interest

According to Mark MacGuigan, Central America — and by extension, El Salvador — is not an area of traditional Canadian interest.[4] Facts tend to belie the Minister's remarks. While it is true that Canadian-El Salvadorean relations have not been as consistently strong as those with some other Caribbean basin states, they do stretch back over half a century.

Canadian engineers, for example, brought the first electricity to the small nation in the 1920s. It was the Montreal-based International Power Company which in 1926 founded *Compañía de Alumbrado Eléctrica* to provide electrical power to the capital, San Salvador. One of the last power systems to remain in private hands in Latin America, International Power was only completely nationalized in 1977.[5]

The most extraordinary chapter in Canadian-Latin American relations was written in January 1932. In that year the dictator General Maximiliano Hernández Martínez had begun the bloody suppression — *La Matanza* — of rebellious peasants. The British Embassy in San Salvador became so concerned about protecting British-owned railways, banks and plantations that it requested protective military intervention by the Canadian Navy.[6]

Two Canadian destroyers, half the entire navy, stopped at the port of Acajutla. HMCS Skeena landed one naval platoon and two Lewis guns. Although the Canadians avoided any direct fighting, their arrival encouraged Hernández Martínez's forces. Naval Commander Victor Brodeur concluded:

> There is no doubt that the presence of ships on the coast strengthened the President's hand considerably, as he immediately started sending troops out of town when he found we were prepared to act in case of emergency. The landing of that platoon had a wonderful moral effect on his troops.[7]

News of the Canadian destroyer's deployment off El Salvador's coast sparked questions in the House of Commons, where J.S. Woodsworth (later a founder of the Cooperative Commonwealth Federation, CCF) demanded to know what the ships were doing. William Lyon Mackenzie King, then leader of the Opposition, wondered out loud whether Canadians were trying "to blast their way into the Latin American markets." After less than a week in El Salvador, the Canadian troops departed since, as it turned out, the dictator Hernández Martínez feared foreign intervention more than the abortive insurrection.

Modern Era

Half a century later, Canadian ties to El Salvador are much less swashbuckling but no less involving. Modern relations are characterized by generous aid and rapidly expanding commerce. During the past decade Canada's trade with El Salvador has grown nearly six fold.

Canadian direct investment, according to the federal government, is worth slightly less than $10 million since International Power's nationalization.[8] The major Canadian corporations with subsidiaries in El Salvador are Moore Corporation, producing business forms, and Canadian Javelin, operating two gold and silver mines.*

More significant than either direct investment or trade is the Canadian aid (mostly tied), which began in the late 1960s. The first major project financed by Canada (through the Canadian fund of the Inter-American Development Bank, IDB) was — ironically — for the redevelopment of the port of Acajutla. Over $5 million was loaned at concessionary terms to modernize the site where Canadian troops had landed in 1932.[9]

In the late 1970s Canada committed over $20 million in grants and low interest loans to the country. The current fighting in El Salvador convinced Canadian officials to withdraw their personnel working on bilateral projects. However, multilateral projects are continuing to be financed. In 1980 this multilateral Canadian funding to El Salvador (through the IDB and the International Monetary Fund, IMF) totaled approximately $3 million.[10] The Washington based Center for International Policy projected similar Canadian financing for 1981-1982 to total $9.7 million.[11]

El Salvador Saga

While statistics testify to the excellence of External Affairs bureaucrats as trade promoters, their uni-dimensional approach has left government policy on El Salvador weak and vulnerable.

In October 1979 a military coup led by younger officers overthrew the regime of General Carlos Romero and installed the first in a series of military-civilian juntas. Canada's response was predictable: it merely endorsed the United States' enthusiasm for a self-styled reformist government offering an alternative to "extremes" of left and right.

Seven months after the coup, in the wake of escalating repression and two successive recompositions of the faltering civilian participation in the junta, Canada's ambassador to Central America, R. Douglas Sirrs, offered the following dispassionate analysis:

> [In El Salvador] you have a situation where it is abhorrent to many
> people outside of El Salvador and in Canada there is tremendous

* Canadian Javelin is run by John Doyle, an entrepreneur with a checkered past who is currently wanted by the RCMP. Doyle escapes arrest by living in Panama.

concern over the bloodshed and the number of people being killed. Sometimes they draw the wrong conclusions. There is an inclination perhaps that decides that the junta is responsible for all this when in fact — to the best of my knowledge — it isn't.

It's trying to balance out the situation and it's almost impossible. You've got violence being precipitated from the extreme right and the extreme left and they are in the middle of it all, and they are being improperly blamed for it by some groups in Canada.

I think this is casting a distortion on it all. That junta, in my view, and many others who are seeking a democratic solution to that problem, see the junta is the only viable alternative . . . that Canada should support and others should support. The other extremes are just not acceptable.[12]

Meanwhile, U.S. President Jimmy Carter was rationalizing the delivery of military supplies to the Salvadorean colonels by recategorizing the aid as "non-lethal". The Canadian Secretary of State for External Affairs, Mark MacGuigan, rose in the House of Commons to defend that action. Dismissing the call of Pauline Jewett (the New Democratic Party External Affairs critic) for a halt to military aid, MacGuigan said: "Our information is that the so-called American aid is purely of a defensive nature."[13]*

Nevertheless, the government came under growing criticism not only from the opposition New Democratic and Progressive Conservative parties but also from individuals, groups, unions and churches across Canada. The November 27, 1980 slaying of El Salvador's leading opposition spokespersons and the rape-murder only six days later of four American missionaries finally forced the Liberal government to act. In an important vote at the United Nations, Canada supported a resolution condemning the human rights violations and urging suspension of military aid to El Salvador.

Canada also challenged the United States by joining some western European nations in opposing an important loan from the Inter-American Development Bank (IDB) to El Salvador. The $45.5 million credit to support the U.S.-designed agrarian reform was approved nonetheless, on the strength of U.S. and Latin American voting power.[14]

Having been lobbied effectively in January 1981, the External Affairs Minister even conceded to meeting with two visiting representatives of the political-diplomatic commission of the FDR/FMLN only four days before his maiden encounter with the newly-installed U.S. Secretary of State, Alexander Haig. MacGuigan received Ana Guadalupe Martínez (a well-known FMLN guerrilla leader) and Hector Oquellí (a member of the social democratic National Revolutionary Movement, MNR) and gave his most hopeful statement yet on Canada's oppositon to American arms shipments to El Salvador. The Minister reiterated Canada's respect

* This aid ranged from tear gas and bullet-proof vests to night-vision scanners developed during the Vietnam war to enable troops to aim their weapons in the dark.

for the principle of non-intervention and self-determination and, in reference to his upcoming meeting with Haig, said: "I'm not sure I will be lecturing him on how the U.S. should behave but I guess he will be able to read between the lines."[15]

Although Canada made no strong public condemnation of U.S. actions in El Salvador, the Minister's meeting with representatives of the FDR/FMLN and his allusion to Ottawa's disagreements with the American State Department spawned expectations of a steady strengthening in Canadian policy. In the midst of Prime Minister Pierre Trudeau's globe-trotting in pursuit of North-South dialogue, it seemed appropriate for Canada to distance itself from Washington's new mood of hostility toward Third World demands. In an interview, MacGuigan appeared to confirm the suggested independence when he offered a warning to the United States:

> The danger is that an American administration might, as some have in the past, tend to see the North-South relationship on the same East-West lines, and to believe that they had to be as hawkish towards countries in the Third World that are not directed by Moscow. I am thinking of countries like El Salvador. We can't forget what happened in Guatemala some years ago when American Marines invaded.[16]

Mr. MacGuigan Goes to Washington

What happened next took most observers by surprise. Mark MacGuigan emerged from his Washington meeting with Alexander Haig and almost completely recanted everything he had earlier said. "I would certainly not condemn any decision the United States takes to send offensive arms [to El Salvador]," the minister told reporters in New York. "The United States can at least count on our quiet acquiescence."[17] Mac-Guigan was the first western ally to be presented with the so-called intelligence material on international Communist subversion in El Salvador. These documents, later to surface as the State Department's controversial "White Paper", caused an abrupt change of heart in the impressionable minister.[18]

Although MacGuigan later claimed that he had been misquoted ("quiescence" versus "acquiescence"), the impression — and reality — remained that Canada had bowed to U.S. pressure.

Churches Attacked

Since the Canadian government was now publicly committed to accept U.S. information on the conflict in El Salvador, the Minister for External Affairs lost no time in attempting to discredit the major alternative viewpoint coming from the Canadian churches. Since before the March 1980 assassination of Archbishop Oscar Romero, the churches had become the leading institutions to challenge the fiction of a "centrist" Duarte government, to document the devastating brutality of the Salvadorean military apparatus and to call for a halt to U.S. arms shipments.

Under attack in the House of Commons for refraining from criticizing the United States, MacGuigan argued that he could no longer accept what the churches told him: "The Canadian churches tell us one thing, the Vatican specifically repudiates what the Canadian Catholic church tells us."[19]

In fact, the Vatican had never made any such contradictory statements. MacGuigan's underhanded attempt to sow division within the Catholic Church fell flat when Bishop Adolphe Proulx, chairman of the Canadian Bishops' Human Rights Commission, said that "neutrality" on El Salvador contravened the Pope's teachings on human rights. Proulx advised Canadians to stay informed and involved and to continue to press the government.[20]

Nevertheless, Ottawa's rapprochement with Washington was quickly enhanced while preparations began for President Ronald Reagan's March 1981 trip to Canada. Not only did the Minister for External Affairs reiterate Canada's refusal to rebuke United States militaristic solutions for El Salvador's crisis, he also made his now famous statement disavowing any Canadian responsibility for action on Central America as a whole:

> I am not aware that we have any serious obligation in that part of the world, in Central America, which is not an area of traditional Canadian interest.[21]

But MacGuigan's disclaimers merely added fuel to the fire of public protest as thousands of Canadians from St. John's to Vancouver prepared national demonstrations to greet Ronald Reagan on his first trip abroad as president.

The several thousand El Salvador and acid rain protesters waving placards in a normally staid Ottawa were characterized by the *Washington Post* as "the most raucous beginning of a trip abroad for an American president since the Viet Nam era".[22]

The final illusions of an independent Canadian foreign policy on El Salvador were laid to rest during MacGuigan's press conference ending the presidential visit. The External Affairs Minister, in his baldest statement to date, summed up the shared viewpoint of Canada and the United States on El Salvador: "There was no difference between the positions of our two governments, and indeed, there was no emphasis in American thought and planning on a military solution."[23] An Ottawa paper offered one particularly trenchant cartoon which encapsulated the whole sorry mess: a militarily outfitted General Haig clutches the shoulder of a diminutive Mark MacGuigan and asks paternalistically, "Now, have you got it straight about El Salvador, MacGuigan?"

Non-Policy Unraveled

Numerous explanations are advanced to explain MacGuigan's embar-
rassing volte-face on El Salvador. Some surmise that the inexperienced
Minister got too caught up in lending credibility to Trudeau's North-
South rhetoric. Others see a cynically-minded Liberal government raising its bargaining leverage with Washington on important issues by
temporarily criticizing U.S. foreign policy. Ottawa's sudden reversal
was purportedly a *quid pro quo* for American concessions on out-
standing problems such as the long-stalled (and now defunct) Fisheries
Treaty. But since there has been no visible headway made on any of
these issues, Canada appears to be bowing unilaterally to American
demands.

This surrender to the United States over El Salvador is symbolic of
External's lack of an over-all policy on Canada's political profile
throughout the hemisphere. Even MacGuigan admits that "Geopoliti-
cally, Canada has been screened from Latin America by the bulk of the
United States."[24]

While Canadian officials lack a coherent plan to promote long-term
Canadian interests, American foreign policy advisers in the Reagan
administration do not. In mid-1980 several "New Right" experts presented then-candidate Reagan with a proposal for U.S. policy toward
Latin America which included recommendations on what responsibilities "Canada must be induced to assume". These Latin
Americanists, two of whom now hold high positions in the Republican
administration, suggested that Canada become more involved in
"extending its influence" throughout the Caribbean basin in alliance
with the United States. "By doing so," their report predicted, "Canada
would become a genuine partner in the hemisphere's security and
growing prosperity."[25]

In early July 1981, as the situation in El Salvador became more
critical, Canada took its cue from Secretary of State Haig and joined the
United States, Mexico and Venezuela in the so-called Nassau Group to
discuss the promotion of stability throughout the Caribbean and Central
America. While Mexico prevented the Americans from excluding Cuba
and Nicaragua from a proposed coordinated aid effort, the "Mini-
Marshall Plan," the United States deftly avoided any mention of its
expanding military aid for El Salvador and other area dictatorships.

Canadian officials later defended the concept of separating questions about military aid from the multilateral aid programme the United
States was sponsoring. R.V. Gorham, External Affairs Assistant Under-
Secretary for Latin America and the Caribbean, told the Parliamentary
subcommittee examining Canada's relations with Latin America and the
Caribbean that "If the United States government wished to supply military assistance to any of these countries, they are entitled to do so, but it
would be completely divorced from this other concept."[26]

MacGuigan's comment on the first meeting of the Nassau Group (named after the site of the four nations' conference) naively endorsed the project: "We think it's a very positive step forward . . . and we're very pleased to be a part of it."[27] But London's *Economist* suggested that the meeting, held only a week prior to the Ottawa western leaders' summit, "was essentially for public relations purposes and to divert attention from America's military aid to El Salvador".[28]

Back in Ottawa, opposition Members of Parliament were dumbfounded by Canadian passivity at Nassau. At a session of the Parliamentary sub-committee on Latin America, Progressive Conservative MP Doug Roche persevered in seeking a straight answer from the senior External Affairs bureaucrat on Latin America:

> Mr. Doug Roche: *The Nassau Communique says, and I am quoting: "The Ministers had full and very cordial discussions of their common concern regarding the economic and social problems facing the countries in the Caribbean and Central America." . . . Are we to understand that El Salvador was not discussed?*
>
> Mr. R.V. Gorham: *As a specific country, no, it was not.*
>
> Mr. Roche: *How would you be able to reconcile the use of that language, that the ministers had a full discussion of economic and social problems in the Caribbean and Central America without having had any discussion of El Salvador?*
>
> Mr. Gorham: *Well, when I say that they did not discuss El Salvador, I mean as a specific problem. I imagine, although I cannot remember the words "El Salvador" were used, that there was certainly . . . a recognition that the problems in Central America particularly had been neglected for far too many years. . . .*
>
> Mr. Roche: *Was there an agreement or any sort of tacit understanding that contentious issues would not be discussed at that conference?*
>
> Mr. Gorham: *Contentious issues?*
>
> Mr. Roche: *And potentially divisive among the four.*
>
> Mr. Gorham: *No, I would not say there was any tacit agreement.*
>
> Mr. Roche: *I would just like to try it on one more time. . . . I have some difficulty getting it straight in my head that a meeting of four foreign ministers on Central America and the Caribbean . . . would not discuss the most visible and contentious example of what happens in the lack of development in a country: El Salvador to wit.*
>
> Mr. Gorham: *I think that was taken as a given. The example was there before us all to see. There was no need to discuss it in detailed terms. . . .*
>
> Mr. Roche: *But there was not an extended discussion at that point?*
>
> Mr. Gorham: *On a particular country?*
>
> Mr. Roche: *On El Salvador.*
>
> Mr. Gorham: *I would not say it was specifically on El Salvador. My memory does not recall that.*
>
> Mr. Roche: *You said . . . that Guatemala was not discussed in a similar vein.*

> Mr. Gorham: *I think Guatemala was mentioned as another example*
> *of the need of social. . . .*
> Mr. Roche: *But in the situation, as such, of how to get economic*
> *and social development going in El Salvador and in Guatemala was*
> *not discussed?*
> Mr. Gorham: *That was not discussed.*[29]

After further questioning, Roche drew the logical conclusion that Canada might have played the hapless pawn at the Nassau summit. Since U.S. military aid was growing more quickly than economic aid, Roche wondered whether "the net effect of this joint effort . . . will have been for Canada to have been used in throwing a cloak of respectability over the continuation of U.S. policy of military aid".[30]

Progressive Options

Must Canada continue to play the role of "Junior Partner" to the United States policy of keeping the lid on in El Salvador?

Ironically, it is Canada's traditional low profile in Latin America, coupled with Prime Minister Trudeau's North-South volubility and the repatriation of Canada's constitution (seen by Latins as symbolic of Canada's independence and coming of age) that gives Ottawa significant credibility throughout the hemisphere. This accumulated (and admittedly undeserved) "political capital" can either be squandered or employed positively.

Ed Broadbent, federal leader of the New Democratic Party (NDP), opened the doors to a positive Canadian role in the El Salvadorean conflict when he travelled in May and June of 1981 to San Salvador and the capitals of the neighbouring states to explore the option of a negotiated settlement. Broadbent's trip, supported by the Socialist International, did not lead directly to mediation between the FDR/FMLN and the junta. However, it did achieve its dual purpose of exposing the destructive futility of present U.S. policy and of highlighting the possibilities of positive contributions by concerned outside parties.

In July 1981 the FDR/FMLN repeated its desire to pursue a "rational method to bring an end to the war and achieve a genuinely pluralistic democracy and social change". This would begin with "a comprehensive process of political negotiation involving the FDR/FMLN and the Salvadorean government" counting on the participation of "a small group of mediators to be selected by both parties".[31] Could Canada act as a mediator, or might the Canadian government lend its official support to an initiative carried out by the NDP?

During 1981 international events pressured the United States to sanction such talks. By recognizing the FDR/FMLN as a "representative political force" in August, France and Mexico built on the Broadbent initiative and refocussed world attention on the need for a political and not an interventionist military solution to the conflict.

Economic Reconstruction

The United States pushed hard for international multilateral financing as a way of getting its allies to join in the hopeless economic bailing-out of the junta. Canada expressed its disagreement with recent IMF and IDB loans to El Salvador, simply because of doubts concerning the technical feasibility of the multi-million dollar projects given present conditions. In December 1980, Canada voted against a $45.5 million IDB loan and in September 1981 it voiced similar reluctance to support a $120 million IMF standby loan.[32] Canada now faces the choice of joining a boycott of all international financing for El Salvador until a political solution is in place.

After that political solution is achieved, enormous infusions of aid will be required to rebuild the shattered and decapitalized El Salvadorean economy. The Canadian government should be able to anticipate providing significant assistance for a newly-established popular government. Planning this kind of programme doesn't have to wait; starting immediately would mean avoiding lengthy delays once a political settlement is reached. After the Nicaraguan insurrection, for example, Canada was completely unprepared to help in the mammoth work of reconstruction.

Conclusions

El Salvador is a relatively close (if often unrecognized) hemispheric neighbour. In September 1981 the El Salvadorean Human Rights Commission reported that 32,000 people had been killed in the twenty-three months since the first military-civilian junta took power. For Canada, a comparable figure would be 160,000 deaths. The Canadian people are rightly interested in promoting a speedy and just resolution of the conflict. On October 31, 1981, an international day of protest against United States intervention in Central America, thousands of Canadians joined in calling for positive Canadian government action on El Salvador.

Just as the deployment of American Green Berets and Huey helicopter gunships in El Salvador conjures up images of Vietnam, so too does the growing strength of the anti-interventionist movement throughout Canada resemble the popular mobilizations of the anti-war protesters over a decade ago. Regardless of the inevitable weakness of official Canadian government policy, it will be the vociferousness of a broadly-based international solidarity movement that will be the critical deterrent to continued American intervention in El Salvador and Central America.

Tim Draimin is editor of Central America Update, *a joint publication of the Latin American Working Group and the Jesuit Centre for Social Faith and Action, both of Toronto.*

Notes

[1] See for example: Heather Robertson, "Canada Hatches a Hawk: Al's Pal", *Today Magazine,* July 18, 1981.

[2] "Canadian Investment, Trade and Aid in Latin America", LAWG *Letter,* May-August 1981, Vol. VII, No. 1/2, p. 25.

[3] The $300 million figure was advanced by Mark MacGuigan, Secretary of State for External Affairs, in a speech to the House of Commons. See *Hansard,* 9 March 1981, p. 8033. That figure represents only the stated "book value" of the investments and some economists estimate the "real value" (including inflation, appreciation, etc.) to be as much as five times that of "book value".

[4] *Hansard,* 2 March 1981, p. 7767.

[5] "Direct Foreign Investment in El Salvador", NACLA *Report on the Americas,* March-April 1980, Vol. XIV, No. 2, p. 31.

[6] *The Globe and Mail,* 11 May 1981.

[7] *Ibid.*

[8] *Hansard,* 16 June 1981, p. 10656.

[9] LAWG *Letter, op. cit.,* p. 34.

[10] *The Globe and Mail,* 10 March 1981.

[11] *Ibid.*

[12] *The San José News,* 23 May 1980, quoted in *Central America Update,* June 1980, p. 117.

[13] *Hansard,* 15 October 1980, p. 3687.

[14] "More Aid in Pipeline", *This Week Central America & Panama,* 5 January 1981, p. 2.

[15] *Canadian Press* (wire service), 26 January 1981.

[16] *Toronto Star,* 31 January 1981. MacGuigan seems to be exaggerating the 1954 Central Intelligence Agency (CIA)-organized coup against the democratically elected government of Jacobo Arbenz. According to most sources, although CIA operatives and some U.S. pilots were involved, no Marines ever landed during the brief overthrow. See: D. Wise & T.B. Ross, *The Invisible Government* (New York, 1974), pp. 165-183.

[17] *The Globe and Mail,* 5 February 1981.

[18] For critiques of the "White Paper" see: "The White Paper on El Salvador: Prelude to U.S. Intervention", *Central America Update,* March 1981, p. 38; James Petras, "Invented Red Menace: White Paper of the White Paper", *The Nation,* 28 March 1981; John Dinges, "Documents Tell Different Tale", *In These Times,* April 1-7, 1981; Jonathan Kwitny, "Tarnished Report?", *Wall Street Journal,* 8 June 1981; Robert G. Kaiser, "White Paper on El Salvador is Faulty", *Washington Post,* 9 June 1981; Wayne H. Cowan, "The Uses of Disinformation", *Christianity in Crisis,* 20 July 1981. For critiques of American press coverage of the affair see: Hodding Carter III, "The El Salvador Crusade", *Wall Street Journal,* 19 March 1981; Jonathan Evan Maslow and Ana Arana, "Operation El Salvador", *Columbia Journalism Review,* May/June 1981; and Claudia Wright, "The Lie Machinery Stirs", *New Statesman,* 1 May 1981.

[19] *Hansard,* 2 March 1981, p. 7766.

[20] *Catholic New Times,*15 March 1981.

[21] *Hansard,* 2 March 1981, p. 7767.

[22] *Washington Post,* 11 March 1981.

[23] *Washington Post,* 12 March 1981.

[24] *Hansard,* 15 June 1981, p. 10610.

[25] Committee of the Santa Fe Council for Inter-American Security, *A New Inter-American Policy for the Eighties* (Washington, 1980), p. 51.

[26] House of Commons, "Subcommittee of the Standing Committee on External Affairs and National Defense on Canada's Relations with Latin America and the Caribbean", Issue No. 12, 16 July 1981, p. 12:101.

[27] *The Globe and Mail,* 13 July 1981.

[28] *Economist,* 18 July 1981.

[29] House of Commons, *op. cit.,* pp. 12:95/96.

[30] *Ibid,* p. 12:105.

[31] July 1981 statement of the FDR/FMLN in reply to a speech by American Assistant Secretary of State for Inter-American Affairs, Thomas Enders, quoted in *Central America Update,* October 1981.

[32] *Latin American Weekly Report* (WR-81-36), 11 September 1981, p. 2.

Bibliography

Allman, T.D., "Rising to Rebellion", *Harper's*, (March 1981).

Anderson, Charles W., *Politics and Economic Change in Latin America: The Governing of Restless Nations*, (Princeton: D. Van Nostrand Company, Inc., 1967).

Anderson, Thomas P., *Matanza: El Salvador's Communist Revolt of 1932*, (Lincoln: University of Nebraska, 1971).

Armstrong, Robert, "El Salvador — Why Revolution", NACLA *Report on the Americas* (Vol. XIV, No. 2, March-April 1980).

Armstrong, Robert and Janet Shenk, "El Salvador — A Revolution Brews", NACLA *Report on the Americas* (Vol. XIV, No. 4, July-August 1980).

Arnson, Cynthia, "Background Information on the Security Forces in El Salvador and U.S. Military Assistance", (Washington, D.C.: Institute for Policy Studies, March 1980).

Arnson, Cynthia and Delia Miller, Update No. 3: "Background Information on El Salvador and U.S. Military Assistance to Central America", (Washington, D.C.: Institute for Policy Studies, June 1980).

Arnson, Cynthia, Update No. 2 and No. 4: "Background Information on El Salvador and U.S. Military Assistance to Central America", (Washington, D.C.: Institute for Policy Studies, November 1980 and April 1981).

Bonner, Raymond, "The Agony of El Salvador", *The New York Times Magazine*, (February 22, 1981).

* Browning, David, *El Salvador: Landscape and Society*, (Oxford: Clarendon Press, 1971).

Browning, David, "The Rise and Fall of the Central American Common Market", *Journal of Latin American Studies*, (Cambridge: Vol. 6, No. 1, 1974).

* Indicates works to which the author is particularly indebted.

Buckley, Tom, "Letter from El Salvador", *The New Yorker,* (June 22, 1981).

Burbach, Robert, "Reading Haig's Secret Documents", *Mother Jones* (June 1981).

Chinchilla, Norma Stoltz, "Class Struggle in Central America: Background and Overview", *Latin American Perspectives* (Vol. VII, No. 2/3, Spring and Summer 1980).

CEPAL, *Notas sobre la economía y desarrollo de américa latina,* (No. 229, diciembre 1976).

CEPAL, *Anuario Estadístico de América Latina,* 1979 (United Nations, December 1980).

Cohen Orantes, Isaac, *Regional Integration in Central America,* (Lexington: D.C. Heath and Company, 1972).

Dalton, Roque, *Las historias prohibidas del pulgarcito* (México: Siglo XXI, 1977).

Dowie, Mark, "Behind the Myth of Land Reform", *Mother Jones* (June 1981).

Dumont, René, *Cuba: Socialism and Development* (New York: Grove Press Inc., 1970).

* Durham, William H., *Scarcity and Survival in Central America,* (Stanford University Press, 1979).

Fuentes, Carlos, "Farewell Monroe Doctrine: A Way Out of El Salvador", *Harper's* (August 1981).

González, Vinicio, "La insurrección salvadoreña de 1932 y la gran huelga hondureña de 1954", *Revista Méxicana de Sociología,* Vol. XL, No. 2, abril-junio 1978).

Gordon, Sara, "Crísis política y organización popular en El Salvador", *Revista Méxicana de Sociología,* (Vol. XLII, No. 2, abril-junio 1980).

Gerassi, John, "America's Hit List. Did the U.S. Make War Inevitable in Central America", *Mother Jones* (June 1981).

* Guidos Véjar, Rafael, *El Ascenso del Militarismo en El Salvador* (San Salvador: UCA/EDITORES, 1980).

Inter-American Development Bank, *Economic and Social Progress in Latin America,* Annual Report 1973, (Washington, D.C.: Inter-American Development Bank, 1973).

Inter-Church Committee on Human Rights in Latin America (ICCHRLA), *Newsletter* (July-August 1980).

Leo Grande, William and Carla Anne Robbins, "Oligarchs and Officers: The Crisis in El Salvador", *Foreign Affairs* (Vol. 58, No. 5, Summer 1980).

Lernoux, Penny, *Cry of the People,* (New York: Doubleday and Co., 1980).

Levin, Jonathan, *The Export Economies: Their Pattern of Development and Historical Perspective* (Cambridge: Harvard University Press, 1960).

Maslow, Jonathan Evan and Ana Arana, "Operation El Salvador", *Columbia Journalism Review,* (May/June 1981).

Matthews, Tom, *et al.,* "Storm Over El Salvador", *Newsweek,* (March 16, 1981).

* Menjívar, Rafael, *Formación y lucha del Proletariado Industrial Salvadoreño,* (San Salvador: UCA/EDITORES, 1979).

Menjívar Larin, Rafael, *El Salvador: El Eslabón Más Pequeño,* (Costa Rica: Editorial Universitaria Centro-americana — [EDUCA], 1980).

Navarro, Vicente, "Genocide in El Salvador", *Monthly Review,* (Vol. 32, No. 17, April 1981).

Richter, Ernesto, "Social Classes, Accumulation, and the Crisis of 'Overpopulation' in El Salvador", *Latin American Perspectives,* (Vol. VII, No. 2/3, Spring and Summer 1980).

Samaniego, Carlos, "Movimiento campesino o lucha del proletariado rural en El Salvador?", *Revista Méxicana de Sociología,* (Vol. XLII, No. 2, abril-junio 1980).

* Simon, Laurence R. and James C. Stephens, Jr., *El Salvador Land Reform, 1980-1981: Impact Audit,* (Boston: OXFAM America, 1981).

Sol, Ricardo, *Para Entender El Salvador* (San José: Departamento Ecuménico de Investigaciones, 1980).

Solorzano Martínez, Mario, "El Papel de la Democracia Cristiana en la Actual Coyuntura Centroamericana", *Estudios Sociales Centroamericanos,* (No. 27, septiembre-diciembre 1980).

Subcommittee on Inter-American Affairs of the Committee on Foreign Affairs, House of Representatives, *Hearings,* March 5 and 11, 1981 (Washington: U.S. Government Printing Office, 1981).

Soto, Max Alberto, "The Labor Markets in Central America", in Juan J. Buttari (ed.), *Employment and Labor Force in Latin America: A Review at National and Regional Levels* (Washington: OAS, 1979).

Torres-Rivas, Edelberto, *Interpretación del Desarrollo Social Centroamericano* (Costa Rica: Editorial Universitaria Centroamericana, 1969).

Torres-Rivas, Edelberto, "The Central American Model of Growth: Crisis for Whom?", *Latin American Perspectives* (Vol. III, No. 2/3, Spring and Summer 1980).

* Webre, Stephen, *José Napoleón Duarte and the Christian Democratic Party in Salvadoran Politics, 1960-1972* (Baton Rouge: Louisiana State University Press, 1979).

Wheaton, Philip, "Agrarian Reform in El Salvador: A Program of Rural

Pacification", (Washington, D.C.: Ecumenical Program for International Communication and Action, 1980).

* White, Alastair, *El Salvador* (New York: Praeger Publishers, 1973).

Wipfler, William L., "El Salvador. Reform as Cover for Repression", *Christianity and Crisis* (Vol. 40, No. 8, May 12, 1980).

Woodward, Jr., Ralph Lee, *Central America: a Nation Divided* (New York: Oxford University Press, 1976).

de Young, Karen, "White Hand of Terror: How the Peace Was Lost in El Salvador", *Mother Jones*, (June 1981).

Periodicals and Newspapers

Central America Update

The Globe and Mail

Latin America Weekly Report (LAWR)

Maclean's

The New York Times

Newsweek

Toronto Star

Appendices

APPENDIX I
Chronology of Events — February 1977-June 1981

Note: this chronology does not attempt to be exhaustive. Rather, it is intended to supplement the book's information on more recent events in El Salvador, in particular to provide greater detail on the persecution of the Church, the composition of the various juntas, the scale of repression and major initiatives taken by the U.S. government, as well as the Canadian response.

February 28, 1977. In Presidential elections held February 20, 1977, "Gen. Carlos Romero became president through the usual electoral fraud. Opposition candidate Col. Ernesto Claramount led a protest demonstration to San Salvador's main square . . . where he told 60,000 supporters he intended to hold a vigil until the national electoral board annulled the results of the fraudulent election. That night [Feb. 28] with 6,000 people still in the plaza, government troops cordoned off the surrounding streets and fired on people who attempted to take refuge in the cathedral. The following day President Romero declared a state of siege. It has been estimated that up to 600 people were killed as a result of the violent repression of this protest." (ICCHRLA, July-August, 1980: 24.)

March 12, 1977. "A Jesuit priest, Father Rutilio Grande, was machine-gunned to death on his way to mass by unknown assailants. His work had radicalized a significant sector of the rural community . . . of Aguilares, located about 20 miles north of San Salvador. . . . The Jesuit's murder was followed by a military attack on the town. . . . The Army called it Operation Rutilio. Simultaneously, the National Guard attacked numerous land occupations in the area, using modern weapons and helicopters to drive workers off the land."

"Aguilares marked a turning point for Archbishop Romero, . . . a conservative when he assumed the position in 1977." (NACLA report, March-April 1980: 24; see also Webre, 1979: 198; ICCHRLA, July-August 1980: 34.)

May 11, 1977. "Father Alfonso Navarro and a boy were assassinated in a parish house in San Salvador." (ICCHRLA, July-August, 1980.)

May 19, 1977. "A military commando in Aguilares attacked the parish church, assassinated a church attendant, desecrated the sanctuary and arrested three priests, who were later expelled from the country." (ICCHRLA, July-August 1980: 34.)

June 1977. "The entire Jesuit order received a death threat; 'leave the country or face extinction', signed, the White Warriors Union." (NACLA report, March-April 1980: 24.)

July 1, 1977. "General Romero was inaugurated president. . . . Since there had been as yet no progress in the [Father Rutilio] Grande case . . . the clergy boycotted the ceremony." (Webre, 1979: 200.)

November 1977. General Romero "attempted to control popular organizations by passing a draconian law which forbade meetings of more than three persons if criticism of the government were the subject of discussion. The law prohibited the distribution of 'false and tendentious' information that would affect adversely the public order. . . . The law, however, had no significant effect on the growth of the popular organizations, which openly defied it. After a year of internal and international pressure, it was repealed in March 1979." (NACLA report, March-April, 1980: 25.)

August 6, 1978. Archbishop Romero, in his Pastoral Letter, supported "the people's right to self-defence 'when a person or a group repel by force aggression they have suffered'. . . . [He] condemned the 'institutionalized violence' which he described as a 'product of an unjust situation in which the majority of men, women and especially children of our country are deprived of the necessities of life'. He went on to say that peasants, workers and people who lived in the poorest neighbourhoods who organized themselves to better their living and working conditions were labelled 'terrorists' and 'subversives', subjected to kidnapping, torture and murder and could not count on the laws or legal institutions to protect them or give them opportunity to defend themselves. Consequently, the Archbishop pointed out, 'they have often been forced to defend themselves to the point of violence, thus encountering once again the arbitrary violence of the state'." (ICCHRLA, July-August 1980: 21.)

December 26, 1978. "A priest Ernesto Barrera Moto was killed, along with other young people, accused of being guerrilla fighters." (ICCHRLA, July-August 1980: 34.)

January 20, 1979. "In a retreat house, Father Octavio Ortiz was assassinated, together with some young people who were spending their first night on retreat." (ICCHRLA, July-August 1980: 34.)

May 1979. "Plainclothesmen from the political police arrested the Secretary General and four principal leaders of the People's Revolutionary Bloc. The Metropolitan Cathedral was occupied in protest. Without warning and in full view of the TV cameras, National Police and Guardsmen opened fire on a crowd gathered on the steps. Twenty-four died." (NACLA report, March-April, 1980: 25.)

June 20, 1979. "The priest Rafael Palacios was murdered in the middle of Santa Tecla Street." (ICCHRLA, July-August 1980: 34.)

August 4, 1979. "Father Alirio Napoleón was assassinated in his own church in San Esteban Catarina." (ICCHRLA, July-August 1980: 34.)

September 1979. "Gen. Romero refused to meet the electoral conditions set down by the major opposition parties and they announced they would boycott the upcoming presidential elections." (ICCHRLA, July-August 1980: 25.)

October 15, 1979. General Carlos Humberto Romero (1977-1979) was overthrown in a bloodless coup organized by a progressive sector of younger officers. To carry out reforms, they organized a five-man civilian military junta composed of: Ramón Mayorga (rector of Catholic University), Guillermo Ungo (Secretary General of the social democratic MNR Party), Mario Andino (representative of the private sector), Colonel Adolfo Majano (an independent and respected officer), Colonel Jaime Gutierrez (a pro-American conservative). A hard-line reactionary Colonel Guillermo García, was appointed Minister of Defense.

The junta's civilian members, however, "did not represent a significant social base. Years of repression and fraud had depleted the ranks of electoral parties, leaving the field to the more militant and radical left: BPR, FAPU, LP. These popular organizations, with memberships in the tens of thousands, were not represented in the newly formed government." (NACLA report, July-August, 1980: 9.)

October 16, 1979. Security forces broke into the locales of "four groups of striking workers in the capital, killing seven, wounding and beating an undetermined number, and detaining 90". (Wipfler, 1980: 119.)

October 21-22, 1979. "In San Salvador, assaults on two mass meetings [left] three dead and several wounded." (Wipfler, 1980: 119.)

October 29, 1979. "A peaceful demonstration . . . called to protest the earlier violence . . . [was] attacked by security forces and result[ed] in 65 persons killed, hundreds wounded and a large number detained." (Wipfler, 1980: 119.)

January 3, 1980. Junta members Ramón Mayorga and Guillermo Ungo, as well as all other civilian members of the cabinet, resign. "Departing officials criticized the 'inclusion in the present government of reactionary forces who are tied in their very roots to the oligarchy, and the failure to achieve closer ties with the popular movements'." (Arnson, June 1980: 4.)

January 9, 1980. A second junta was organized following the January 3 resignations of the civilian members of the first junta. Christian Democrats replaced those who left. This new junta included "the original two colonels, Majano and Gutierrez, two Christian Democrats — Hector Dada Hirezi [an economics professor and Minister of Foreign Affairs under the first junta], and Antonio Morales Ehrlich [Secretary-General of the PCD and a Vice-Presidential candidate in the 1977 elections] and Dr. José Ramón Avalos, a physician, an independent". (ICCHRLA, July-August 1980: 28.)

January 10, 1980. "The FPL, the RN and the Communist Party announced the formation of a co-ordinating council of the political-military organizations." (NACLA report, July-August 1980: 11.)

January 11, 1980. The United Popular Action Front *(Frente de Acción Popular Unificada* - FAPU), the Popular Revolutionary Bloc *(Bloque Popular Revolucionario* - BPR) and the Popular Leagues - 28th of February *(Ligas Populares 28 de Febrero* - LP-28), "in combination with the Democratic Nationalist Union (UDN), a Marxist Party that had been invited to participate in the cabinet of the first junta, reached a compromise on their political differences and signed a declaration of unity.... The new coalition was called the Movement of National Unity and an ongoing structure composed of the top leadership of the previous organizations was established as the Revolutionary Coordination of the Masses the [*Coordinadora*]." (Wipfler, 1980: 120.)

January 22, 1980. "[O]nly 11 days after its formation, the *Coordinadora* risked a public show of strength, organizing a peaceful march through the capital city of San Salvador.... [T]he demonstrators walked ten-abreast in a procession 62 blocks long. Estimates of the numbers varied from 300,000 by the *Coordinadora* to 50,000 by the Government and U.S. Embassy. Before the BRP, the largest of the mass organizations, had joined the march, snipers fired on the crowd, killing 20 people and dispersing the participants." (Wipfler, 1980: 121.)

January-February 1980. "The Legal Aid Office [of the office of the Archbishop] documented the assassination of over 600 people [during the two months], among them 255 peasants, 26 students and 17 workers." (Wipfler, 1980: 121.)

February 10, 1980. "Ten students between the ages of 13 and 19 were killed by a police attack on a peaceful demonstration. A march had been organized by MERS (secondary school section of BPR)."

"On the same day ... the National Police and the Treasury Police attacked the headquarters of the Christian Democratic Party which had been occupied for fifteen days by representatives of the LP-28. Three LP-28 members were killed during the initial assault. The occupation had been peaceful and the PDC had not requested any action from the police forces. There were approximately fifty people on the second floor, LP-28 members and their hostages.... [They] were taken downstairs and made to lie face down on the floor. The police asked the members of the LP-28 to identify themselves and the few that did ... were killed in cold blood, some with long knives like machetes. Some of the hostages described the slaughter as 'horrendous'. Twenty of the LP-28 members were arrested and turned over to the Fifth Criminal Court." (ICCHRLA, July-August 1980: 29.)

Mid-February 1980. Roberto D'Abuisson, an ex-intelligence officer with close ties to the military and extreme right-wing groups and death squads, "appeared on Salvadorean TV to denounce a list of persons who, he said, were linked to the political-military organizations of the left. Among them was Mario Zamora Rivas, then Solicitor General of the second junta. Zamora was a bridge between the left and right wings of the Christian Democratic Party. Destroying that bridge might force the party out of the junta. Several nights later, armed men entered Zamora's house through the roof and killed him with a tommy gun. The Christian Democrats ... pointed the finger at D'Abuisson and threatened to re-sign if Zamora's killers were not brought to justice. But no one was arrested and the Christian Democrats stayed on." (NACLA report, July-August 1980: 14.)

February 17, 1980. "Archbishop Romero announced that he had writ-ten a letter to President Carter, asking the United States to stop sending military assistance to El Salvador because it would be used to intensify repression against the people, and to guarantee that the U.S. would not intervene 'in the determination of the future of the Salvadorean peo-ple'." (ICCHRLA, July-August 1980: 29.)

February 18, 1980. "Two bombs completely destroyed the transmitters and antennae of the Archdiocesan radio station. At the same time, another bomb destroyed the library of the Central American University (a Jesuit university)." (ICCHRLA, July-August, 1980: 30.)

February 23, 1980. "Archbishop Romero denounced the cruel repres-sion suffered by the peasants in Aguilares and Suchitoto settlements 33 and 48 kilometers north of the capital. During the period between Feb-ruary 1-23 there had been five military invasions of peasant settlements in the Aguilaras, Suchitoto, San Vicente, Zacatecoluco and La Unión areas, resulting in the deaths of at least fifty peasants. During these invasions, they literally occupied a zone for a period of at least five days. They were sometimes accompanied by members of ORDEN who brought with them lists of names of people active in the peasant organi-zations. What follows is a campaign of terror during which homes are burned, young girls raped and peasants murdered in the presence of their families, or abducted and later found dead, their bodies showing unmistakeable signs of torture." (ICCHRLA, July-August 1980: 30.)

March 3, 1980. Hector Dada Hirezi resigned from the second junta. In a letter of resignation, he explained: "The junta is incapable of taking action against those whom I see as the principal opponents of the process of reform, and it is clearer every day that they are firmly ensconced in the very structures of the government. . . . We have not been able to stop the repression, and those committing acts of repression in defiance of the junta's authority remain unpunished; the promised dialogue with the popular organizations has not come about; the possibilities of generating reforms supported by the people have retreated beyond our grasp." (ICCHRLA, July-August 1980: 31.)

March 5, 1980. José Napoleón Duarte accepts to replace the vacancy in the second junta left by the resignation of Hector Dada Hirezi.

March 6, 1980. A three phase agrarian reform programme was announced (see Appendix IV). On the same day, a state of siege was declared, suspending free speech, freedom of the press, right to public assembly and the right of habeas corpus.

March 10, 1980. "Popular faction of the Christian Democratic Party withdr[ew] from the party at the national convention, claiming that 'the Christian Democratic Party should not participate in a regime which has unleashed the bloodiest repression ever experienced by the Salvadorean people. . . . The 600 victims of repression between January and February clamor for justice'. The faction held 20% of the convention's delegates." (Arnson, June 1980: 4.)

March 10, 1980. "Seven members of the leadership of the Christian Democratic Party, including Alberto Arene, Rubén Zamora, Roberto Lara Velado, Hector Silva, Francisco Díaz Rodríguez, Francisco Raniagua, and Hector Dada, resign[ed] from the Party. [They stated]: . . . Respect for human rights is incompatible with the exacerbated and growing repression exercised against the popular organizations and against the people in general . . . a program of reforms with repression runs contrary to the fundamentals of Christian Democracy'." (Arnson, June 1980: 4.)

March 22, 1980. "The National Police encircled UCA (the University of Central America), went inside the campus, killed a male student and imprisoned a female student." By this time, the UCA had been "the object of a dozen bombings". In the first months of 1980 there had been two: "one on January 22 and one during the night of March 18-19". (ICCHRLA, July-August 1980: 34.)

March 23, 1980. Archbishop Romero, in his Sunday homily, "urged the Salvadorean soldiers to obey the laws of God and to disobey officers who ordered them to kill their brothers". (ICCHRLA, July-August 1980: 22.)

March 24, 1980. Archbishop Oscar Arnulfo Romero was shot dead while saying Mass. "The judge in charge of the investigation declared before the Tribunal [of the Peoples, Mexico City, February 9-17, 1981] that the Archbishop was murdered by the security forces with the knowledge of and acceptance by the armed forces and by the junta. Because of his knowledge of these facts, the judge's life was threatened by the security forces; and, after an attempt on his life, he had to escape the country." (Navarro, 1981: 3.)

The judge then issued a "report on his investigation into the assassination from Panama. The report implicates two men who are known to be involved in the leadership of the para-military right wing groups. . . . One is Gen. Alberto Medrano and the other Major (ret.) Roberto D'Abuisson who was chief of the Political section of the Intelligence Department (G2) of the National Guard, under the regimes of Colonel Molina and General Romero." (ICCHRLA, July-August 1980: 32.)

March 26, 1980. Jorge Villacorta, Under-Secretary of Agriculture, Oscar Menjívar, Minister of Economy, and Eduardo Colinders, Minister of Education resigned from the government. Villacorta explained: "This war, whose dead are in the majority peasants or militants of popular organizations, reflects who the security forces and sectors of the Army consider their principal enemies. . . . With these crimes, the effects of the agrarian reform are lost." (Arnson, June 1980: 4.)

April 9, 1980. Roberto Solorzano, Deputy Minister of the Economy, resigned. (Arnson, June 1980: 4.)

April 18, 1980. "The Democratic Revolutionary Front (FDR) was formed . . . when the Revolutionary Coordinating Council of the Masses (CRM), representing all the popular organizations, united with the Democratic Front (FD). The FD was a newly formed organization composed of trade unions, professional organizations, small business groups, student associations, the two major universities and, most significantly, the social democratic MNR and the Popular Social Christian Movement [a new group composed of the Christian Democrats who left the junta in March]." (NACLA report, July-August 1980: 23-24.)

April 29, 1980. Roberto Alvergue Vides, Minister of Finance, resigned because he "did not agree with decree No. 207 [governing the expropriation of leased lands] of the junta which harms the small agricultural properties and which has stunned the campesinos even more." (Arnson, June 1980: 4.)

Roberto Suarez Suay, Minister of the Presidency, also resigned "in protest over the junta's inability to stem the violence afflicting the nation". (Arnson, June 1980: 4.)

April 30, 1980. Roberto Salazar Candell, Minister of Planning, resigned. "Criticizing junta member José Napoleón Duarte Salazar stated that 'the Christian Democratic Party endangers the economic stability of the country by passing laws for propaganda purposes abroad'." (Arnson, June 1980: 4.)

May 7, 1980. "Major D'Abuisson was arrested in El Salvador along with several other officers and civilians, accused of trying to organize a coup d'état. Within three days of his arrest, the junta had given in to pressure to release him, despite the fact that two junta members and the United States Ambassador to El Salvador, Robert White, had publicly accused Major D'Abuisson of trying to organize a coup. He had incriminating documents in his possession when arrested and had made and had used tape recordings and video tapes in an attempt to incite the Army into overthrowing the government. The same day that Major D'Abuisson was released from custody, Colonel Abdul Gutierrez replaced Colonel Adolfo Majano as the 'strong man' of the Armed Forces." (ICCHRLA, July-August 1980: 32-33.)

Key officers backing Majano were subsequently transferred to new postings to neutralize their command over troops reportedly loyal to Majano. Eight of the fourteen army barracks in the country had been considered sympathetic to Majano. . . . The transfers were ordered by the right-wing Minister of Defense, Colonel García, and supported by the junta member Colonel Gutierrez. The two men are the key components of a right-wing consolidation within the armed forces. (*Central America Update*, October 1980: 14.)

May 1980. Carlos Cordero D'Abuisson, Minister of Foreign Trade, resigned. (Arnson, June 1980: 4.)

May 14-15, 1980. Rio Sumpul Massacre. Approximately 600 peasants, including women, children and the elderly were killed while attempting to cross the Sumpul River to Honduras. Honduran as well as Salvadorean troops took part in the massacre.

June 2, 4, 8, 1980. "Peasant settlements in various regions were invaded by security forces, often accompanied by units of ORDEN. Many peasants were robbed, injured or killed. In the incident of June 8, 3,000 members of the Army, National Guard and ORDEN attacked 29 peasant settlements in the San Vicente region. Two helicopters and two other airplanes tracked down fleeing peasants." (ICCHRLA, July-August 1980: 33.)

June 1980. "The Democratic Revolutionary Front (FDR) called for a general strike that was almost textbook perfect in its execution. Eighty per cent of El Salvador's businesses were closed down. The city of San Salvador was deserted. Even non-union factory workers, court and bank employees, and government agronomists joined the strike." (NACLA report, July-August, 1980: 25.)

June 5, 1980. Eight provincial executive councils of the Unión Salvadoreña Comunal (UCS) signed a letter protesting the violence sparked by the land reform. The UCS, a peasant organization, was founded by the American Institute for Free Labor Development (AIFLD), an international project of the AFL-CIO. It is now funded by the U.S. Agency for International Development (AID) and receives additional support from almost 100 multinational corporations.

July 11, 1980. "103 peasants from the San Vicente and Morazán regions crowded into the Costa Rican embassy in San Salvador. They did not hold Ambassador Alvaredo Piza or any of his staff hostage. Instead they presented the ambassador with a six-page document addressed to the governments of Mexico, Spain, Italy, Panama, Costa Rica and Venezuela, requesting asylum and asking those governments to use their influence to get a commission of inquiry into the repression in El Salvador set up by the United Nations Human Rights Commission, Amnesty International and the International Red Cross. They emphasized the importance of such a commission going into the countryside." (ICCHRLA, July-August 1980: 33.)

Mid-July 1980. "A FDR delegation . . . visited Canada for a week, meeting with government officials, MPs and leading Church and trade union figures. During their visit . . . the FDR received strong endorsation from both church and labor. The government made no commitments regarding the recognition of a state of belligerency in El Salvador [a preliminary step towards recognition of the FDR] but has begun to make representations to the junta regarding the human rights situation." (*Central America Update*, August 1980: 2.)

August 13-15, 1980. "El Salvador was gripped by a general strike called by the Democratic Revolutionary Front (FDR). Reports indicate that the shutdown was 80 per cent successful in the countryside with 70 per cent of urban production closed. The important port of Acajutla was also completely paralyzed."

"In well coordinated military actions, the security forces were mobilized throughout the countryside and the capital to intimidate strikers. The resulting fighting is estimated to have cost nearly 300 lives."

"Government troops militarized public transportation — actually going to bus owners' homes and forcing them to operate. The junta also employed a new law which makes public workers liable for dismissal if absent from work for two days." (*Central America Update*, August 1980: 1.)

August 21, 1980. "Electrical workers occupied nine power-generating plants and cut off electricity to the entire country. The shutdown, which caused millions of dollars damage in lost production, was to protest the firing of 35 workers and the generalized atmosphere of repression. Within 36 hours well-armed troops backed by armoured cars had forcibly succeeded in taking back five of the struck plants." (*Central America Update,* August 1980: 1.)

August 22, 1980. "Over 100 leaders and rank and file members were arrested in the largest sweep of trade unionists in recent Salvadorean history. . . . Almost the entire leadership of the STECEL union [electrical workers] was arrested, as well as the Secretary General of the FENASTRAS [National Federation of Salvadorean Workers], Hector Bernabe Recinos." (*Central America Update,* October 1980: 12.)

August 23, 1980. "The junta completed its offensive against the country's outspoken trade unions by 'militarizing' the plants in which they work. According to a newly passed decree law, all employees at the Sub-ministry of Water (ANDA), Communication (ANTEL), Electrical Energy (CEL), and Ports (CEPA) have been drafted into the Armed Forces, and will be forced to work under military supervision." (*Central America Update,* October 1980: 12.)

October 3, 1980. "Maria Magdalena Henríques of the Salvadorean Human Rights Commission was captured by people dressed in civilian clothes. Her body was discovered four days later 33 km. outside the capital. On the same day the body of Father Manuel Rafael Reyes was found. Reyes had been picked up earlier by the National Police." (*Central America Update,* October 1980: 14.)

January 5 - October 10, 1980. "Twenty-eight members of the Church hierarchy and its lay persons were assassinated (including the Archbishop) and 21 were detained, with 14 bombings, 41 machine-gunnings, 18 attacks, 15 robberies, 33 seizures of churches, religious residences, religious schools and other religious institutions." (Navarro, 1981: 3.)

October 12, 1980. "Mon. Rivera y Damas condemns the assassination of Rev. Manuel Monico after his arrest by government troops. Monico was the 10th cleric to be killed by rightists since 1977. The Archbishop states in his weekly homily that 'the repression from the military and the right against our people and their church, is [carried out] with impunity'." (Arnson, November 1980: 6.)

October 15, 1980. "The government junta announces on the first anniversary of the coup that elections for a constituent assembly will be held in 1982, and for a civilian government in 1983." (Arnson, November 1980: 6.)

October 24, 1980. "The Treasury Police opened fire on a group of people who were performing a comic play which was critical of the government, in the street; they killed 30 players and bystanders and wounded dozens more." (ICCHRLA, July-August 1980: 27.)

October 26, 1980. "Ramón Valladares, administrator of El Salvador's Human Rights Commission, is assassinated by unidentified gunmen." (Arnson, November 1980: 7.)

November 27, 1980. "Six members of the FDR's executive committee including its president, Enrique Alvarez Córdoba, were abducted in San Salvador . . . and their tortured bodies were found the next day.

"Other FDR victims include Juan Chacón, General Secretary of the People's Revolutionary Bloc; Enrique Barrera, leader of the National

Revolutionary Movement, Doroteo Hernández, leader of an organization of shanty-town dwellers, ... Humberto Mendoza, leader of the Movement for Popular Liberation, and Manuel Franco, General Secretary of the Nationalist Democratic Union. The abductions took place in broad daylight after 180 uniformed police and guardsmen had surrounded the San José High School where the FDR executive was meeting in the offices of the Legal Aid Department of the Arch-Diocese of San Salvador." (*Central America Update,* December 1980: 17.)

December 1, 1980. "Four American missionaries, Ursuline sister, Dorothy Kazel and laywoman Jean Donovan, both from Cleveland, and Maryknoll sisters, Ita Ford and Maura Clarke from New York, [were] assassinated by the National Guard." (*Central America Update,* December 1980: 18; see also *The Globe and Mail,* August 21, 1981.)

December 2, 1980. "As a result of growing public pressure from across Canada, the Secretary of State for External Affairs has been forced to make public statements indicating the government's opposition to direct foreign intervention in El Salvador. The Minister has also gone on the record stating that Ottawa would regard any supply of military aid by outside power as an intrusion in the internal affairs of El Salvador." (*Central America Update,* December 1980: 20.)

December 5, 1980. "The Carter administration condemned the assassinations of the American church women and announced that it would suspend all military and economic aid to the Salvadorean junta. The suspension applies to $20 million in economic aid and $5 million in military sales for ... [1980], but will not stop delivery of such equipment as 75 two-and-a-half ton trucks that had already been contracted for." (*Central America Update,* December 1980: 18; See also Cynthia Arnson "In El Salvador, Why Back Regime Based on Violence?" *Los Angeles Times,* Monday December 8, 1980.)

December 13, 1980. José Napoleón Duarte is named president of the junta and Colonel Jaime Abdul Gutierrez is named Vice-President. These were new titles.

January 3, 1981. Michael Hammer and Mark Pearlman, who worked as agrarian reform consultants with AIFLD, together with José Rodolfo Viera, the head of the Institute of Agrarian Transformation, were killed in San Salvador.

January 17, 1981. U.S. President Carter authorized an emergency $5 million shipment of lethal military aid to El Salvador.

January 26, 1981. External Affairs Minister MacGuigan "met in Ottawa with representatives of the Democratic Revolutionary Front (FDR) and expressed Canada's opposition to foreign intervention in El Salvador". Ana Guadalupe Martínez, a member of the joint committee of the FDR/FMLN, and Hector Oquelí, a former foreign minister of El Salvador, visited Ottawa as a part of an international tour which included visits to

West Germany, Austria, and other European nations. They sought Canada's initiative in opposing foreign intervention, including military aid to El Salvador and also Canada's willingness to express to the U.S. the openness of the FDR/FMLN to negotiate with the U.S. (*Central America Update*, March 1981: 36.)

January 28, 1981. "Alexander Haig said at a press conference that 'international terrorism will take the place of human rights' on the list of U.S. concerns." (*The Washington Post,* February 14, 1981.)

January 30, 1981. After having a brief meeting in Washington with U.S. Secretary of State Alexander Haig, External Affairs Minister MacGuigan made the following statement: "I would certainly not condemn any decision the United States takes to send offensive arms there [to El Salvador]. . . . The United States can at least count on our quiet acquiescence." (*Central America Update,* March 1981: 36.)

February 2, 1981. "Top U.S. diplomats in El Salvador have objected to a Washington proposal to send more military advisers to the beleaguered Central American country. . . . However, they expect the Pentagon to get its way. There are now 23 U.S. military advisers in El Salvador, and one source says the Defense Department wants to send an additional 55 advisers." (*Newsweek,* February 2, 1981.)

February 19, 1981. "The State Department released a summary of 'incontrovertible' information which reconstructs 'the central role played by the Communist countries and several radical states in the political unification, military direction and arming of insurgent forces in El Salvador'." (*Central America Update,* March 1981: 39.)

February 19, 1981. "Venezuela begins distancing itself from the U.S. and its foreign minister, José Alberto Zambrano, criticizes the U.S. for turning Latin America into terrain for its confrontation with the Soviet Union." (*Central America Update,* March 1981: 39.)

February 19, 1981. "In repeated statements the FDR/FMLN emphatically denies that it has received arms from the governments of Vietnam, Ethiopia, Cuba, Russia or any other governments." (*Central America Update,* March 1981: 39.)

February 23, 1981. The Reagan Administration released a special White Paper entitled "Communist Influence in El Salvador". The paper purported to show "indirect Communist aggression" and Soviet support of the Revolution. Later the *Wall Street Journal* and other independent evaluators of the paper point out that the evidence (allegedly captured documents) does not support the conclusions.

February 23, 1981. "Mexico's President José López Portillo criticizes efforts to resolve El Salvador's internal crisis by military means and argues that only a political settlement could prevent the conflict from spreading elsewhere in Central America." (*Central America Update,* March 1981: 39.)

February 23, 1981. "Speaking to the *New York Times,* the Salvadorean opposition renews its offer to negotiate a political settlement." (*Central America Update,* March 1981: 39.)

March 2, 1981. "The U.S. announces it will send 20 more military advisers to El Salvador as well as $25 million in additional military aid. According to the State Department this will raise to 45 the number of U.S. military personnel in the country. The FDR, however, claims there are already 230 U.S. soldiers there." (*Central America Update,* March 1981: 40.)

March 3, 1981. "Bernt Carlsson, the Secretary General of the Socialist International meets in Washington with U.S. State Department officials to offer the mediation services of Willy Brandt to begin talks with President Reagan. The FDR/FMLN have already accepted the SI's mediation offer." (*Central America Update,* March 1981: 40.)

March 5, 1981. "President Duarte establishes an electoral council in preparation for the election of a constituent assembly in 1982." (*Central America Update,* March 1981: 40.)

March 11, 1981. "External Affairs Minister MacGuigan asserts that 'the present government is probably the most feasible channel through which the people of El Salvador can realize democracy'." (*Central America Update,* March 1981: 41.)

Beginning of March, 1981. "The civil-military junta, bolstered by a fresh supply of U.S. armaments, launched a major counter-insurgency campaign in the northern provinces of Morazán, Chalatenango, Cuscatlán and Cabañas."

"This offensive, inspired by instructions received from the 56 American military advisers in El Salvador, was designed to destroy the guerrilla units in the area and to cut the FMLN off from its base of support among the local population." (*Central America Update,* June 1981: 48.)

March 15, 1981. "The Salvadorean military, employing a force of 1500 soldiers and members of ORDEN, surrounded 9 insurgent-controlled towns in the province of Cabañas. There were approximately 10,000 civilians in the area when the attack began. After three days of fighting, guerrilla units managed to break through the government encirclement. Before retreating, the insurgents organized the evacuation of some 7-8,000 women, children and elderly. As these refugees tried to cross the Rio Lempa into Honduras, two Salvadorean jet fighters and a U.S.-supplied helicopter bombed and strafed them while Honduran and Salvadorean ground troops fired from both sides of the river. At least 50 people were killed by drowning or in direct hits before the fleeing peasants could reach safety." (*Central America Update,* June 1981: 49.)

March 27, 1981. In the province of Morazán, 1,500 children, young women and elderly people caught in the middle of a "search and destroy" operation of the Salvadorean military took refuge in a series of caves near the Honduran border. "The soldiers pursuing them tossed tear gas cannisters into the caves to flush them out. Those who tried to escape the gas were gunned down by the awaiting Salvadorean troops. The peasants too frightened to leave the caves died of asphyxiation." (*Central America Update,* June 1981: 49.)

April 7, 1981. "Security forces entered the slum district of Monte Carmelos in San Salvador and killed thirty civilians in cold blood." (*Central America Update,* June 1981: 49.)

April 7, 1981. "Reinaldo Erazo, rector of the Superior Teachers' College in the Honduran capital of Tegucigalpa, denounced the bombing of refugees in grottos known as La Pintada, . . . about two km. from the border in the Salvadorean province of Morazán." (*The Globe and Mail,* June 2, 1981.)

May 7, 1981. "New Democratic Party Leader Edward Broadbent [announced his intention] to visit Central America and the U.S. as an emissary of the Socialist International to find a 'political solution' to the war in El Salvador. The decision to send Mr. Broadbent on the peace mission was taken by the Socialist International during a meeting . . . in Amsterdam." (*The Globe and Mail,* May 7, 1981.)

May 29, 1981. Salvador's president, José Napoleón Duarte, rejected Broadbent's mediation effort and stated: "We made clear that to accept a mediation in the affairs of the country would be to accept an act of intervention." He added: "We told our distinguished visitor that the most adequate political solution to the Salvadorean conflict is the electoral process." (*Toronto Star,* May 29, 1981.)

June 5, 1981. Edward Broadbent presented his Salvadorean peace proposals to the State Department, but "the U.S. government refused to make the radical foreign policy changes the New Democratic Party leader believes are necessary to end the bloody civil war in El Salvador". Broadbent predicted that elections scheduled for 1982 and 1983 in El Salvador "would be a travesty of the norms of justice" given the state of civil war in the country. (*The Globe and Mail,* June 6, 1981.)

APPENDIX II

The Security and Paramilitary Forces, U.S. Involvement With the Security Forces*

* Reproduced from: Cynthia Arnson, "Background Information on the Security Forces in El Salvador and U.S. Military Assistance" and Update No. 4 (Washington, D.C.; Institute for Policy Studies, March 1980, and April 1981).

THE SECURITY FORCES

The official government security forces consist of the Army, the Navy and the Air Force; all are under the direction of the Minister for Defense and Public Security. Three paramilitary units — the National Guard, the

National Police and the Treasury Police — are also under the direction of the Defense Ministry and are usually commanded by Army officers. An additional unit, the Customs Police, is under the jurisdiction of the Department of the Treasury. The Territorial Service, made up of Army reservists, numbers about 75,000. Its membership overlaps with that of ORDEN *(Organización Democrática Nacionalista)*, a paramilitary unit under the Ministry of Defense and by custom headed by the President of the Republic.

The Army
With 6,500 men and five infantry regiments, the Army is the largest official state security organization. Its Chief of General Staff commands all other armed forces units. Besides providing for "external defense", the Army "is charged with assisting in the maintenance of public order and participating in civic action". The Territorial Service is directly under Army jurisdiction.

The Navy
Formed in 1952 out of the Coast Guard, the El Salvadorean Navy of 130 men has coastal patrol and search and rescue responsibilities. With only four small patrol boats, the Navy has little combat capability.

The Air Force
Consisting of 300 men, the Air Force was designed to support ground troops through aerial surveillance, airdrop, resupply and transport.

The National Guard
Created in 1912 by Spanish officers, the National Guard functions as a militarized police force, with detachments in most rural towns and villages. With approximately 2,500 men, it is organized into five commands with regional headquarters throughout the country. The National Guard, essential in maintaining political control in rural areas, has normally been under the direction of an Army major.

The National Police
Numbering about 1,900 men, the National Police is responsible for "law and order" in urban areas and for criminal investigations throughout the country. It works in close collaboration with the National Guard and the military. The Investigative Division of the National Police constitutes the country's intelligence unit, and investigates political as well as criminal cases.

The Treasury Police
With about 660 men, the Treasury Police serves as a support force for the National Guard and the National Police. It also has responsibility for customs duties. In this capacity, it is aided by the Customs Police, numbering about 530, with border control and narcotics control duties.

PARAMILITARY SECURITY FORCES
ORDEN *(Organización Democrática Nacionalista)*
Founded in 1968 by General José Alberto Medrano "to make a barrier

to the attempts of the communists to provoke subversion in the country-side", ORDEN is a civilian paramilitary organization of 50,000-100,000 which enjoyed full government support. Its members were authorized to carry firearms and often worked in collaboration with government security forces, in addition to engaging in violent and repressive measures of their own. ORDEN was formally prohibited by Decree Law 12 of the first civilian-military junta that overthrew General Romero. General Medrano has called for its reconstitution, however, as the National Democratic Front.

White Warrior's Union *(Union Guerrillera Blanca* — UGB)
The UGB is a right-wing terror squad which threatened in 1977 to execute all Jesuit priests in the country for being "communists". The UGB is believed to have links to the Eastern Region Farmer's Front (*Frente de Agricultores de la Región Oriental* — FARO), a landowners' organization instrumental in blocking the implementation of the Agrarian Reform Act of 1976.

Anti-Communist Armed Forces of Liberation — War of Elimination
(Fuerzas Armadas de Liberación Anticommunista — Guerra de Eliminación — FALANGE)
FALANGE is a right-wing death squad consisting of active, retired, or off-duty members of the security forces.

Organization for the Liberation from Communism *(Organización para la Liberación del Communismo* — OLC)
Created after the overthrow of Romero, the OLC stated in a February communiqué that "The Communists and their followers are our country's worst enemies. Our entire war is aimed at them and we are willing to offer our lives in the course of this war."

U.S. INVOLVEMENT WITH EL SALVADOR'S SECURITY FORCES
From the turn of the century until immediately after World War II, Chilean officers directed military training and operations for the Salvadorean armed forces. Chileans founded the first War College, later renamed the Command and General Staff School, and directed its activities until 1957. U.S. training and doctrine became increasingly important following World War II, when El Salvador received its first U.S. grants under the Military Assistance Program, as well as the first U.S. military mission.

Security assistance from the United States to El Salvador between Fiscal Year 1950 and Fiscal Year 1979 has totalled $4.97 million in Military Assistance Program grants, $3,479 million in Foreign Military Sales Agreements, $2,454 million in Excess Defense Articles, and $5,814 million in International Military Education and Training Program grants, all for a total of $16.72 million. The United States has trained a total of 1,971 Salvadorean officers, including at least 17 in Urban Counterinsurgency, 14 in Military Intelligence, 108 in Basic Combat and Counterinsurgency and 124 in Basic Officer Preparation.

According to the Pentagon in 1977, "our security assistance program facilitates our overall relations with the government of El Salvador and fosters useful professional contacts with key members of the Salvadorean armed forces".

Internal Security and U.S. Office of Public Safety (OPS)
To upgrade El Salvador's police and internal security forces, the United States instituted in 1957 a Public Safety programme under the auspices of the Agency for International Development, "to develop the managerial and operational skills and effectiveness of its civil police forces". Between 1957 and the programme's termination in 1974, OPS spent a total of $2.1 million to train 448 Salvadorean police, and provide arms, communications equipment, transport vehicles, and riot control gear.

Until 1962, the programme was directed mainly at the National Police; from 1963 on, the programme's emphasis shifted to the National Guard. At the height of U.S. involvement between 1963 and 1965, five U.S. advisers were stationed in the country to oversee training and programme management. When Congress terminated the OPS programme in 1974, U.S. AID analysts concluded that "The National Police . . . had advanced from a non-descript *cuartel*-bound group of poorly trained men to a well-disciplined, well-trained and respected uniformed corps. It has good riot control capability, good investigative capability, good records, and fair communications and mobility. It handles routine law enforcement well."

Graduates of OPS training, including those brought to the United States for studies at the International Police Academy (IPA) in Washington, D.C., occupied key positions in the Salvadorean security establishment. The assistant to the head of the Intelligence Division of the National Police was an IPA graduate; at various times the top positions in the Treasury Police, the Customs Police, and Immigration were U.S.-trained, as were the second- and third-in-command in other security agencies.

Public safety advisers reorganized the Police school, prepared a standard textbook for the Treasury Police, and trained and equipped special riot control units in the National Police and National Guard. OPS created within the National Police a bomb-handling squad "responsible for investigating terrorist activities", established a central police records bureau, and installed a teletype system linking El Salvador, Nicaragua, Honduras, Guatemala, Costa Rica and Panama. Funds provided under OPS were used to purchase 2,045 revolvers and carbines; 94 transport vehicles, including jeeps, sedans, and trucks; 208 mobile radio units and base radio stations; 755,000 rounds of ammunition; 950 tear gas grenades and projectiles; and assorted other riot control helmets, handcuffs, training films, camera and narcotic test kits.

ARMS SALES
Until the mid-1970s, the El Salvadorean armed forces were equipped

primarily with surplus U.S. equipment, largely from World War II stocks, including three T-34, ten T-6, and six T-41 trainers, and six C-47 helicopters. In 1975 the Israeli and El Salvadorean governments concluded a package deal to re-equip the Salvadorean Air Force. Israeli sales of 18 refurbished French Fighter bombers and trainers were the first jet aircraft operated by the Salvadorean Air Force. Since the Israeli sales in 1975, France has sold several more trainers, as well as light tanks, and the state-owned Brazilian firm EMBRAER has concluded a sale of twelve patrol aircraft, which use U.S.-designed engines and radar.

In 1977, El Salvador joined Argentina, Brazil and Guatemala in rejecting proposed U.S. military assistance, in protest over U.S. criticism of its human rights record. No new requests for assistance were made in Fiscal Years 1979 or 1980, although deliveries of previously-authorized equipment and training have amounted to at least $1.04 million since 1978.

Arms sales by private U.S. firms, which must be licensed by the State Department's Office of Munitions Control, have totalled $2.0 million since Fiscal Year 1971. Increasingly, U.S. companies have been selling to private guard services in El Salvador, as well as to traditional security forces.

U.S. Arms Policy to March 1980
On November 9, 1979, the U.S. government authorized a sale of $205,541 of tear gas, gas masks, and protective vests to El Salvador's security forces. Three days later, for a cost of $7,176, a six-man U.S. military training team arrived in El Salvador to train security forces in riot control. Between October 1, 1979 and December 31, 1979, El Salvador used $213,000 in Foreign Military Sales credits and purchased $801 worth of weapons through the Commercial Sales programme.

On December 14, 1979, the Defense Department informed Congress of its intent to reprogramme $300,000 in International Military Education and Training grants from Fiscal Year 1980 funds for El Salvador. These funds, which are now available to be spent, would go primarily for the purchase of U.S. Mobile Training Teams, placing U.S. military personnel in El Salvador for training purposes. On March 4, 1980, the Defense Department informed Congress of an additional reprogramming of $5.7 million in Foreign Military Sales credits for El Salvador. Congress has fifteen days in which to act on the Administration's recommendation; otherwise, the reprogrammings become effective. In Fiscal Year 1981, the Administration is asking for an additional $5 million Foreign Military Sales credits and $498,000 in training grants, bringing total proposed assistance (reprogramming plus new funds) to a total of $11.5 million, or 69% of all military assistance El Salvador has received since 1950. With no further authorizations of U.S. money, El Salvador still has $472,000 "in the pipeline" from authorizations from previous years.

Referring to the proposals for security assistance to El Salvador, Archbishop Oscar Romero, in a letter to President Carter in mid-February (1980), stated that "The contribution of your government, instead of favoring greater justice and peace in El Salvador, undoubtedly will sharpen the repression." Referring to the November tear-gas sale, Romero charged that "The security forces, with better personal protection and effectiveness, have repressed the people even more violently using deadly weapons."

THE CARTER INHERITANCE

On January 17, 1981, three days before President Carter left office, his administration authorized an emergency $5 million shipment of lethal weapons to El Salvador. "We must support the Salvadorean Government," announced the State Department, "in its struggle against left-wing terrorism supported covertly with arms, ammunition, training, and political and military advice by Cuba and other Communist nations." Authority to send the aid — which did not require Congressional approval — came under Section 506(a) of the Foreign Assistance Act, which allows the President to send aid if "an unforeseen emergency exists which requires immediate military assistance."

The Carter Administration, in its last weeks in office, also leased 6 Bell UH-IH helicopters to El Salvador, restored $5 million in Fiscal Year 1981 credits suspended after the murder of four U.S. churchwomen, and authorized the placement of up to 20 U.S. military trainers in El Salvador (not including the staff of the U.S. Military Group stationed at the Embassy in San Salvador).

Part of the justification for increasing military aid was the announcement by the Salvadorean guerrillas (*Frente Farabundo Martí de Liberación Nacional* — FMLN) of a major military offensive beginning in mid-January. Also important were the first U.S. accusations of substantial foreign involvement in El Salvador's war. On January 14, then-U.S. Ambassador Robert White claimed that "circumstantial . . . but compelling and convincing evidence" existed of Nicaraguan material support for Salvadorean rebels. "I believe the reports," he stated, "that approximately 100 men landed from Nicaragua. . . .We can't stand idly by and watch the guerrilla movement receive outside assistance."

In response to these accusations, the Carter administration suspended disbursement of the remaining portion of a $75 million aid package to Nicaragua approved by Congress in 1980.

THE REAGAN OFFENSIVE

It was the Reagan administration, however, that catapulted El Salvador into the headlines as a crisis of international proportions. In early February, the State Department and Pentagon began to leak portions of allegedly captured documents detailing Soviet, Cuban, and Eastern bloc support for the Salvadorean guerrillas. On February 10th, administration officials said that a $9.6 million wheat sale to Nicaragua was being held up pending review of Nicaragua's involvement in El Salvador.

Then, in a special briefing on El Salvador on February 17th, Secretary of State Alexander Haig told NATO representatives that "a well orchestrated international Communist campaign designed to transform the Salvadorean crisis from the internal conflict to an increasingly inter-nationalized confrontation is underway. With Cuban coordination, the Soviet Bloc, Vietnam, Ethiopia and radical Arabs are furnishing at least several hundred tons of military equipment to the Salvadorean leftist insurgents. Most of this equipment, not all but most, has entered via Nicaragua."

The same day, designated-Deputy Secretary of State William Clark told Latin American diplomats that "we intend to go to the source with whatever means may become reasonably necessary" to stop the arms flow from Cuba. The warning was repeated by Edwin Meese, Reagan's White House foreign policy adviser. Asked about the possibility of a U.S. naval blockade of Cuba, Meese replied, "I don't think we would rule out anything."

By the time State Department officials publicly released on February 23 a special report entitled "Communist Influence in El Salvador", along with an inch-thick volume of supporting documents, high level diplomatic missions had been dispatched to Western Europe and Latin America to seek allied support for U.S. policy.

Additional Emergency Aid

Within days after releasing the documents, the Reagan administration announced major new increases in military assistance for El Salvador. A Pentagon assessment of the El Salvadorean Army had reportedly con-cluded in late February that the armed forces were "not organized to fight a counterinsurgency war", and had "no hope" of defeating the guerrillas with existing resources. The National Security Council met on February 27th, and approved the placement of additional U.S. non-combat advisers in El Salvador, as well as the provision of additional material.

The proposals were spelled out at a State Department briefing on March 2, 1981. They included:
* $25 million in Foreign Military Sales credits and loan guarantees to "permit the Government of El Salvador to acquire additional helicop-ters, vehicles, radar and surveillance equipment and small arms", and
* Four additional five-man teams to "train Salvadorean personnel in communications, intelligence, logistics, and in other professional skills designed to improve their capabilities to interdict infiltration and to respond to terrorist attacks".

$20 million of the arms credits came from a military aid contingency fund allowing the President to bypass Congress in sending emergency aid to foreign countries. Another $5 million was "reprogrammed" from

Fiscal Year 1981 funds, and required Congressional approval. The Senate Appropriations Subcommittee on Foreign Operations approved the reprogramming on March 13. The House Appropriations Subcommittee on Foreign Operations approved the aid on March 24.

U.S. Military Personnel in El Salvador

As of late March, 1981, the Reagan administration had authorized the placement of 56 U.S. military personnel in El Salvador for training and administrative purposes. Their functions were as follows:

6 — Staff of U.S. Military Group at the U.S. Embassy (raised from a level of 4);

5 — Mobile Training Team acting as an adiunct to the MilGroup, for administrative, logistics, and command purposes related to the presence of additional U.S. personnel;

6 — naval training team "to assist the Salvadorean Navy in improving its capability to interdict seaborne infiltration of arms destined for the leftist guerrillas" and to "survey the need for upgrading and refurbishing Salvadorean patrol boats and provide training in the maintenance of boats and other naval equipment."

14 — training in the use and maintenance of helicopters;

15 — three small unit training teams of five men each to "provide in-garrison training for the Salvadorean's new quick-reaction force". The 15 are counter-insurgency specialists from the U.S. Army School of Special Forces, who had been stationed in Panama. They will provide basic, air mobile tactics, and counter-insurgency tactics training. The "quick reaction force" envisioned by the Salvadoreans involves an infantry unit of 2,000 men supported by helicopters for rapid mobility to points of conflict;

10 — two "operational and planning assistance teams" of five men each to aid each of El Salvador's five regional commands in planning specific operations. (One of these teams, authorized under Carter, was involved in "Operation Golden Harvest" — protecting the harvest against guerrillas.)

56   TOTAL

The War Powers Act and Other Legislation

The Reagan Administration has taken care to point out that "U.S. personnel will not accompany Salvadorean units outside their garrison areas. Nor will U.S. personnel participate in any combat operations." Nevertheless, numerous members of Congress have charged that the Administration has not adequately consulted Congress, and that the decision to send military personnel may be a violation of the War Powers Act of 1973. The Act requires that Congress be notified in writing within 48 hours of any situation " . . . in which United States forces are introduced into hostilities, or into situations where imminent involvement in hostilities is clearly indicated by the circumstances."

A section of the Arms Export Control Act, moreover, requires that "... personnel performing defense services ... may not perform duties of a combatant nature, including any duties related to training and advising that may engage United States personnel in combat activities...."

In early March, 45 members of the House of Representatives telegrammed President Reagan advising him that "... any involvement of military personnel in hostilities in El Salvador requires compliance with the War Powers Act." Senator John Glen (D-OH), member of the Senate Foreign Relations Committee, has said he will "closely watch" Administration compliance with the War Powers Act and the Arms Export Control Act.

Under pressure from Congress and the U.S. press to the effect that the presence of U.S. military advisers in El Salvador could lead to another Vietnam-like entanglement, the Reagan administration indicated in late March that most or all of the U.S. military personnel could be withdrawn from El Salvador by summer or fall of 1981. On March 13th, however, Under Secretary of State for Political Affairs Walter Stoessel Jr. told a Senate Subcommittee that "... El Salvador is not another Vietnam.... Experience has shown, however, that for our support to be credible, it must respond not only to the present situation but to the potential of the other side to create further violence.... We must anticipate future needs rather than being merely reactive. There is, thus, an element of deterrence built into our support."

PROPOSALS: FISCAL YEAR 1982

"Throughout Latin America, internal pressures for change continue to build. Uncontrolled change, however, is destabilizing and can create a climate favorable for exploitation by outside powers. In Central America, popular demands for social and economic reform, dwindling U.S. influence, and expanding Cuban and Soviet influence and presence all converge to accelerate the prospects for turmoil."

General David C. Jones. USAF, Chairman of the Joint Chiefs of Staff

El Salvador and Honduras

In Fiscal Year 1982, the Reagan administration has proposed dramatic increases in military aid to El Salvador and Honduras. The Pentagon is requesting for *El Salvador* $25 million in Foreign Military Sales (FMS) credits, $1.0 million in International Military Education and Training (IMET) grants, and $40 million in Economic Support Funds (ESF — see below); all this is *over and above* the $25 million in emergency aid sent to El Salvador in early March, 1981. Thus, in the space of two years, the United States has *increased aid to El Salvador 400%* over the total sent between 1950 and 1979.

Honduras is slated to receive an additional $10 million in FMS credits and $0.7 million in IMET funds, a doubling of the request during the last year of the Carter administration. As of March, 1981, two Mobile Training Teams of two men each were active in Honduras.

Economic Support and Special Requirements Funds

The Reagan administration has also requested substantial increases for "special requirements funds" designed to give the Executive discretionary power to send aid in international emergencies. One such channel — Economic Support Funds (ESF) — differ from military aid in the strict sense in that they are not intended to purchase weapons. Rather, they finance projects that will "enhance a nation's security" — for example, the building of bridges, roads, etc. In addition, these monies address emergency needs — for food, medical supplies, or balance of payments support.

Of the $250 million requested for Economic Support Funds in Latin America, only $120 million is assigned to particular countries, leaving a $130 million ESF "slush fund" for the region.

The second category of "special requirements" reinstates the Military Assistance Program (MAP) — the grant portion of military aid phased out in Latin America during the Carter administration. The Pentagon has requested $100 million in MAP funds, none of which is assigned to a particular country. Thus, the Reagan administration has asked Congress for a total of $230 million in wholly discretionary funds (ESF and MAP combined) in Fiscal Year 1982 for Latin America alone. It is entirely likely that *Guatemala,* for which there is no specific Pentagon request, will benefit under these programmes.

Military Aid Legislation

Several members of the House of Representatives and the Senate are sponsoring legislation to terminate or condition U.S. military aid to El Salvador. The major bills include:

H.R. 1509, introduced by Rep. Gerry Studds (D-MA), with 80 co-sponsors (March 30, 1981). The bill would terminate all military assistance and sales to El Salvador;

S728, introduced by Sen. Edward Kennedy (D-MA), with 4 co-sponsors. The bill would prohibit military assistance and the presence of U.S. military personnel in El Salvador unless the President reports that: there is a thorough investigation of the murder of U.S. citizens in El Salvador; civilians have a role in decision making and leadership; there is an investigation of the acts of murder committed by Salvadorean security forces; (partial list of conditions);

A bill introduced by Reps. Jonathan Bingham (D-NY) and Stephen Solarz (D-NY) in the House, and Sen. Chris Dodd in the Senate, to suspend all military assistance and withdraw all U.S. advisers unless the President certifies that the Salvadorean government: is not engaged in human rights violations, has achieved control of the security forces, is continuing to implement political and economic

reforms, is committed to holding free elections, and has demonstrated a willingness to seek a negotiated political resolution of the
conflict.

APPENDIX III

*The following "Programmatic Platform of the Revolutionary Democratic Gov-
ernment" was made public by leaders of the Coordinadora Revolucionaria de
Masas (CRM — Revolutionary Coordinating Committee of the Masses) at a news
conference in San Salvador on February 27, 1980.
The text is from the March 4 and 5 issues of *Barricada,* published in Managua.
The translation is by *Intercontinental Press.*

The Program of the Revolutionary Opposition*

The economic and social structures of our country — which have
served to guarantee the disproportionate enrichment of an oligarchic
minority and the exploitation of our people by Yankee imperialism —
are in deep and insoluble crisis.

The military dictatorship is also in crisis, and with it the entire legal
and ideological order that the oligarchic interests and the U.S.
imperialists have defended and continue to defend, oppressing the Salvadoran people for half a century. Victims of their own contradictions,
the dominant classes have failed due to the decisive and heroic action
of the people's movement. It has been impossible to stave off this failure, even with the more and more brazen intervention of the United
States in support of such efforts against the people.

Unswerving commitment to the interests and aspirations of the Salvadoran people by the revolutionary organizations has led to the deepening and strengthening of their roots among the vast toiling majority
and the middle sectors. Being so rooted in the people, the revolutionary
movement is now indestructible. It constitutes the only alternative for
the Salvadoran people, who can be neither stopped nor diverted from
their struggle to gain a Free Homeland in which their vital desires will
be made real.

The economic and political crisis of the dominant classes on the one
hand, and on the other the forward impulse of the decisive political
force in our country, the people's movement, have given rise to a revolutionary process and to conditions in which the people can assume
power.

The revolutionary transformation of our society — submitted up to
now to injustice, betrayal, and pillage — is today a near and possible
reality. Only in this way will our people gain and insure the democratic
rights and freedoms that have been denied to them. Only the revolution
will resolve the agrarian problem and generate for the masses of peasants and agricultural wage workers material and spiritual conditions of
life favorable to the immense majority of our population who are today
marginalized and submerged in poverty and cultural backwardness. It

will be the revolution that will gain true political independence for our country, giving the Salvadoran people the right to freely determine their destiny and attain true economic independence.

This revolution is therefore popular, democratic, and anti-oligarchic, and seeks to conquer true and effective national independence. Only the revolutionary victory will halt the criminal repression and make it possible for the people to enjoy the peace that today they lack, a solid peace based on freedom, social justice, and national independence.

The revolution that is on the march is not, nor can it be, the work of a group of conspirators. To the contrary, it is the fruit of the struggle of the entire people — of the workers, the peasants, the middle layers in general, and all sectors and individuals that are honestly democratic and patriotic.

The most conscious and organized ranks of the Salvadoran people, now multitudinous, are fighting in a more and more broad and united way. The worker and peasant alliance — through its combativity, level of consciousness, daring, organization, and spirit of sacrifice for the sake of the people's triumph — has proven to be the most solid basis for guaranteeing the firmness and consistency of the entire liberation movement. Expressing the unity of the entire people, this movement unites the revolutionary forces and the democratic forces — the two great torrents generated by the long struggle carried out by the Salvadoran people.

The decisive task of the revolution on which completion of all its objectives depends is the conquest of power and the installation of a *revolutionary democratic government* which at the head of the people will launch the construction of a new society.

Tasks and Objectives of the Revolution

The tasks and objectives of the revolution in El Salvador are the following:

1. To overthrow the reactionary military dictatorship of the oligarchy and Yankee imperialism, imposed and sustained against the will of the Salvadoran people for fifty years; to destroy its criminal-political military machine; and to establish a *revolutionary democratic government*, founded on the unity of the revolutionary and democratic forces in the People's Army and the Salvadoran people.

2. To put an end to the overall political, economic, and social power of the great lords of land and capital.

3. To liquidate once and for all the economic, political, and military dependence of our country on Yankee imperialism.

4. To assure democratic rights and freedoms for the entire people — particularly for the working masses, who are the ones who have least enjoyed such freedoms.

5. To transfer to the people, through nationalizations and the creation of collective and socialized enterprises: the fundamental means of pro-

duction and distribution that are now hoarded by the oligarchy and the U.S. monopolies, the land held in the power of the big landlords, the enterprises that produce and distribute electricity and other monopolized services, foreign trade, banking, and large transportation enterprises. None of this will affect small- or medium-sized private businesses, which will be given all kinds of stimulus and support in the various branches of the national economy.

6. To raise the cultural and material living standards of the population.

7. To create a new army for our country, one that will arise fundamentally on the basis of the People's Army to be built in the course of the revolutionary process. Those healthy, patriotic, and worthy elements that belong to the current army can also be incorporated.

8. To encourage all forms of organization of the people, at all levels and in all sectors, thus guaranteeing their active, creative, and democratic involvement in the revolutionary process and securing the closest identification between the people and their government.

9. To orient the foreign policy and international relations of our country around the principles of independence and self-determination, solidarity, peaceful coexistence, equal rights, and mutual respect between states.

10. Through all these measures, to assure our country peace, freedom, the well-being of our people, and future social progress.

The Democratic Revolutionary Government — Its Composition and Platform of Social, Structural, and Political Changes

The revolutionary democratic government will be made up of representatives of the revolutionary and people's movement, as well as of the democratic parties, organizations, sectors, and individuals who are willing to participate in the carrying out of this programmatic platform.

This government will rest on a broad political and social base, formed above all by the working class, the peasantry, and the advanced middle layers. Intimately united to the latter forces will be all the social sectors that are willing to carry out this platform — small- and medium-sized industrialists, merchants, artisans, and farmers (small- and medium-sized coffee planters and those involved in other areas of agriculture or cattle raising). Also involved will be honest professionals, the progressive clergy, democratic parties such as the MNR [*Movimiento Nacionalista Revolucionaria* — Revolutionary Nationalist Movement], advanced sectors of the Christian Democracy, worthy and honest officers of the army who are willing to serve the interests of the people, and any other sectors, groups, or individuals that uphold broad democracy for the popular masses, independent development, and people's liberation.

All these forces are now coming together to make up a revolutionary and democratic alliance in which the political and/or religious beliefs of all are respected. The organized form to be taken by this voluntary alliance at the service of the Salvadoran people will be the result of consultations among all those who make it up.

Immediate Political Measures

1. A halt to all forms of repression against the people and release of all political prisoners.

2. Clarification of the situation of those captured and disappeared since 1972; punishment of those responsible (be they military or civilian) for crimes against the people.

3. Disarming and permanent dissolution of the repressive bodies — ANSESAL, ORDEN, National Guard, National Police, Treasury Police, and Customs Police, along with their respective "Special sections"; of the Gotera "Counterinsurgency School" and the so-called Armed Forces Engineering Training Center in Zacatecoluca; of the cantonal and suburban military patrols; of the oligarchy's private paramilitary bands; and of all other kinds of real or nominal organizations dedicated to criminal action or slander against the people and their organizations. The current misnamed security bodies will be replaced by a civilian police force.

4. Dissolution of the existing state powers (executive, legislative, and judicial); abrogation of the Political Constitution and of all decrees that have modified or added to it.

The *revolutionary democratic government* will decree a constitutional law and will organize the state and its activities with the aim of guaranteeing the rights and freedoms of the people and of achieving the other objectives and tasks of the revolution. In doing so, the *revolutionary democratic government* will adhere to the United Nations' "Universal Declaration of Human Rights."

The constitutional law referred to above will remain in force while the Salvadoran people prepare a new Political Constitution that faithfully reflects their interests.

5. Municipal government will be restructured so as to be an organ of broad participation by the masses in managing the state, so as to be a real organ of the new people's power.

6. The *revolutionary democratic government* will carry out an intense effort of liberating education, of cultural exposition and organization among the broadest masses, in order to promote their conscious incorporation into the development, strengthening, and defense of the revolutionary process.

7. The People's Army will be strengthened and developed. It will include the soldiers, noncommissioned officers, officers, and chiefs of the current army who conduct themselves honestly, reject foreign intervention against the revolutionary process, and support the liberation struggle of our people.

The new army will be the true armed wing of the people. It will be at their service and absolutely faithful to their interests and their revolution. The armed forces will be truly patriotic, the defenders of national sovereignty and self-determination, and committed partisans of peaceful coexistence among peoples.

8. Our country will withdraw from CONDECA [Central American

Defense Council] from TIAR [Rio de Janeiro InterAmerican Defense Treaty], and from any other military or police organizations that might be the instruments of interventionism.

9. The revolutionary democratic government will establish diplomatic and trade relations with other countries without discrimination on the basis of differing social systems, on the basis of equal rights, coexistence, and respect for self-determination. Special attention will be paid to the development of friendly relations with the other countries of Central America (including Panama and Belize), with the aim of strengthening peace and upholding the principle of nonintervention. Close fraternal relations with Nicaragua will especially be sought, as the expression of the community of ideals and interests between our revolution and the Sandinista revolution.

Our country will become a member of the Movement of Nonaligned Countries and will develop a steadfast policy toward the defense of world peace and in favor of détente.

Structural Changes
The revolutionary democratic government will:

1. Nationalize the entire banking and financial system. This measure will not affect the deposits and other interests of the public.

2. Nationalize foreign trade.

3. Nationalize the system of electricity distribution, along with the enterprises for its production that are in private hands.

4. Nationalize the refining of petroleum.

5. Carry out the expropriation, in accord with the national interest, of the monopolistic enterprises in industry, trade, and services.

6. Carry out a deepgoing agrarian reform, which will put the land that is now in the hands of the big landlords at the disposal of the broad masses who work it. This will be done according to an effective plan to benefit the great majority of poor and middle peasants and agricultural wage workers and to promote the development of agriculture and cattle raising.

The agrarian reform will not affect small and medium landholders, who will receive stimuli and support for continual improvements in production on their plots.

7. Carry out an urban reform to benefit the great majority, without affecting small and medium owners of real estate.

8. Thoroughly transform the tax system, so that tax payments no longer fall upon the workers. Indirect taxes on widely consumed goods will be reduced. This will be possible not only through reform of the tax system, but also because the state will receive substantial income from the activity of the nationalized sector of the economy.

9. Establish effective mechanisms for credit, economic aid, and technical assistance for small- and medium-sized private businesses in all branches of the country's economy.

10. Establish a system for effective planning of the national economy,